THEME·EXPLORATION

A Voyage of Discovery

- Constance Weaver
- Joel Chaston
- Scott Peterson

Scholastic Canada Ltd.

Scholastic Canada Ltd.
123 Newkirk Road, Richmond Hill, Ontario, Canada L4C 3G5

Scholastic Inc.
730 Broadway, New York, NY 10003, USA

Ashton Scholastic Limited
Private Bag 1, Penrose, Auckland, New Zealand

Ashton Scholastic Pty Limited
PO Box 579, Gosford, NSW 2250, Australia

Scholastic Publications Ltd.
Villiers House, Clarendon Avenue, Leamington Spa, Warwickshire
CV32 5PR, UK

Cover design by Yüksel Hassan, photo © First Light/Larry Lee

Canadian Cataloguing in Publication Data

Weaver, Constance
    Theme exploration: a voyage of discovery

Includes bibliographical references.
ISBN 0-590-73460-1

1. Elementary school teaching. I. Chaston, Joel.
II. Peterson, Scott, 1949-. III. Title.

LB1027.W42 1993   371.3'32   C93-093503-9

6 5 4 3 2 1   Printed in USA   3 4 5 6 7 8/9

~ ~ ~

As our theme exploration project developed, several other people became involved in it with us. In particular we want to acknowledge:

Nora Wolf, a first-grade teacher at Ezard Elementary School in Conway, Missouri, who has conscientiously and successfully adopted whole language principles in her teaching, and who welcomed Joel into her classroom.

Vickie Atkinson, who at the time of the project was working on a degree in elementary education and serving as an aide in Nora's classroom.

Tom Coder, who, out of a lingering desire to teach, volunteered to help in Scott's classroom, and who enjoyed the project so much that he has decided to pursue a career in teaching.

~ ~ ~

Acknowledgements

The authors and publisher wish to thank the following copyright holders for permission to quote specific passages:

From *Gates of Excellence* by Katherine Paterson, © 1981 by Katherine Paterson. Used by permission of Lodestar Books, an affiliate of Dutton Children's Books, a division of Penguin USA Inc.

From *The Island* by Gary Paulsen. Copyright © 1988 by Gary Paulsen. Used by permission of the publisher Orchard Books, New York.

From *A Ring of Endless Light* by Madeleine L'Engle. Copyright © 1980 by Crosswicks Ltd. Reprinted by permission of Farrar, Straus and Giroux, Inc.

From *When Writers Read* by Jane Hansen, published by Heinemann, a Division of Reed Publishing (USA) Inc., Portsmouth, NH, 1987. Reprinted by permission of Jane Hansen.

From *The Whole Language Evaluation Book*, edited by Kenneth Goodman, Yetta Goodman and Wendy Hood, published by Heinemann, a Division of Reed Publishing (USA), Inc., Portsmouth, NH, 1989. Reprinted by permission of Kenneth Goodman.

~ ~ ~ ~ ~ ~ ~

Table of contents

~ ~ ~ ~

~ ~ ~ ~ ~

Introduction

~ ~ ~ ~

This book contains the story of a theme exploration project that grew. It grew from a simple upper elementary theme unit into a teacher/researcher study of theme exploration in whole language classrooms, with a focus on the first and fourth grades. In fact, the book grew too, from the intended two authors to three.

All three of us are growing into whole language teaching, and to us, exploring a theme with students seems the epitome of whole language teaching. It's the most appropriate way to actualize some of the principles of whole language, particularly the principle that students develop language and literacy best when using language to gain understanding of a wide range of topics, themes and concepts.

Our understanding of the effectiveness of theme exploration wasn't instinctive, however; in large part, it grew out of our experience with this project. As a result, this book is an intensely personal one, the closest thing to confessional writing we have ever published. We could assign blame (or as least responsibility) for this tone to our editor, Adrian Peetoom. But we have to admit that we found it salutary, even satisfying, to make public our shortcomings as well as our strengths. We're learning to allow ourselves, as well as others, to be human.

We all too frequently hear people speak of whole language in "either/or" terms — either you're a whole language teacher or you're not. We've even contributed to this unproductive dichotomizing in an attempt to clarify the nature of whole language. Realistically, though, we have yet to meet anyone who is wholly a whole language teacher, if by that we mean someone who adheres *all of the time* to *all of the principles* that constitute a whole language philosophy of education — as if anyone could delineate "all" of the principles, anyway!

Most of the whole language teachers we know are still, in many respects, walking and talking contradictions, ourselves included. Even the best are still growing into the philosophy, still striving to implement its principles as those principles evolve, still trying to bring their teaching into line with their beliefs about learning. Maybe a reasonable description of a whole language teacher is this: *someone who continually strives to implement the best that is known about how to foster learning and who, by being a reflective practitioner, contributes to that ever-growing, ever-changing understanding.* If this is a fair characterization of a whole language teacher, then we would like to consider ourselves whole language teachers!

The language in this book is personal because we know that one of the best ways for teachers to grow professionally is to share with one another. We have benefitted from others sharing with us their excitement and successes, their despair and defeats. Now we want to share ours — including our false starts, partial successes and embarrassing contradictions. We hope that this account of our human failings will make it easier for others to take risks and struggle their way into becoming more fully whole language teachers.

The rewards of writing about our experiences have been immense. While we considered ourselves reflective practitioners throughout the project, the process of collaborating on writing the book has extended our own understanding considerably beyond what it was when the two classroom projects officially ended.

Who we are

Connie Weaver is a professor of English at Western Michigan University. In light of her recently published *Understanding Whole Language,* her lapses from "ideal" whole language practice may seem disconcerting, yet we hope that including them will provide comfort to other teachers. Her own continuing need to learn and grow became the reason for this project.

Joel Chaston, a former colleague of Connie's now teaching at Southwest Missouri State, is a children's literature expert. Connie lured him into the project with a blithe promise of eventual publication, not mentioning — not knowing! — that publication would be four years away.

Scott Peterson, a fourth-grade teacher, has 20 years of teaching practice behind him. He has chalk dust in his veins, and his hands are permanently stained with magic marker. Believing that teachers must constantly grow and change to meet the challenges of educating children for the 21st century, Scott is excited by the research emerging from the whole language movement.

Our voyage of discovery

The "voyage of discovery" alluded to in the title refers to the growth each of us experienced as we participated in this theme exploration project, a "journey" Connie already anticipated in a journal entry she wrote as she contemplated the project before it began:

> We feel that by moving away from externally imposed expectations towards the interests and needs of those in the classroom, we are moving towards the true center of the curriculum: children. We believe also that by moving from the role of traditional teacher more and more towards that of whole language teacher, we are approaching the center of what it means to *be* a teacher. And certainly we are moving towards the center of ourselves, as we confront who we are and what we believe, and as we try to minimize the

contradictions between what we believe and what we do as professionals . . .

Part of what I shall confirm for myself, I think, is that I am forever a discoverer . . . I can readily identify with the Ulysses in Tennyson's poem, who claims, even as his life draws to a close: "I cannot rest from travel; I will drink / Life to the lees." I, too, feel my spirit "yearning in desire / To follow knowledge like a sinking star, / Beyond the utmost bound of human thought." The knowledge for which I yearn is not exclusively of the intellect, however, but also of the heart and spirit. And I foresee that as we approach the centers that we seek, we will find that the center is not a static entity, but a fluid process of change and rediscovery, an infinitely receding shore . . .

And in that spirit we set forth upon our voyage of discovery.

~ ~ ~ ~ ~ ~ ~ ~ ~ ~ ~

Embarking on our journey

~ ~ ~ ~ ~ ~

Connie ~ From theme unit to theme exploration

Joel, Scott and I took different routes to a holistic philosophy of learning and teaching, as our three stories clearly demonstrate. Mine was initially an intellectual journey.

I had already acquired three degrees in English and American literature, and all of my professors had taken for granted the prevailing notion that meaning is *in* the text, ready to be pried out. Eventually, however, research began to focus on the importance of a reader's prior knowledge. I was excited and challenged by the notion that reading is an intellectually active process, and that readers must *construct* meaning, not pry it from the text.

After several years of studying cognitive development, language acquisition and the reading process, I began to accept on an emotional level what I increasingly understood intellectually. I began to really believe that children are not blank slates waiting to be written upon by adults. They learn primarily through their own cognitive efforts, drawing on their interactions (transactions) with others and with the external environment to construct their own reality. I began to realize that children are *always* in control of their own learning, no matter what or how we teach, or what we demand as evidence that they have learned. Whether or not they give back on tests or papers what we have taught, what they have *actually* learned (if anything) is entirely within their control.

As a result, my own college teaching began to change. Gradually I began to let go of my control over what my students were reading and writing, and encourage them to assert a greater degree of ownership over how they demonstrated what they had learned. For several years now, as a final exam, my students have described what they've learned, focusing on what's most important to them personally and using virtually any format they choose: a letter or imaginary exchange of letters, a play, a myth or fable, an original story or a parody, even an original newspaper or magazine. These two factors — choice of what to emphasize and how to convey it — have made an incredible difference in the quality of final exam papers I receive.

Even so, I soon realized that simply allowing the students to take ownership of and responsibility for their own learning wasn't enough. It occurred to me that I still needed to give guidance, that in my writing process course, for example, I could and should "teach" technique and/or immerse the students in literature that would give them models to select from. I no longer believed in the kind of assignment that asks students to immediately practice new techniques and demonstrate their mastery. I began, instead, to provide examples of effective techniques that could be drawn upon or not as the students chose. Now my teaching reflects an awareness that both teacher *and* students contribute significantly to learning. For the present, I am comfortable there.

Though this contrast between then and now may seem trivial, I have come to understand that it indicates a profound difference between underlying concepts of education. What I did in the past reflected a *transmission* concept: teach something, have students practice it, then test to see that the "something" has been mastered. Simply adding a particular technique to the hoard of possible techniques reflects a *transactional* concept: the teacher demonstrates something and invites learners to try it but doesn't insist that they immediately practice it or give evidence of learning. Obviously, whole language reflects a transactional concept of learning.

(For a more detailed account of my growth toward and understanding of the whole language philosophy, see my *Understanding Whole Language: From Principles to Practice.*)

The robot unit

It was at this point in my growth toward whole language that I encountered the next challenge to my understanding: an opportunity to discover the meaning behind the phrase "negotiating the curriculum," which had become almost a cliché in whole language circles.

I had become interested in the Science, Technology and Society movement, which seeks to support the development of "technological literacy." Like those active in that movement, I believe that people should be informed about science and its technological impact upon society and human life in order to make informed decisions as citizens. This interest led to my decision to present a unit on robots at a whole language conference in Winnipeg sponsored by a group known as C.E.L. (Child-centered Experience-based Learning).

Frankly, I didn't know what else to do. Without asking my preferences, the conference organizers had scheduled me for a two-and-a-half-hour presentation to teachers of grades four to six. I sensed that they wanted something "practical" — something the teachers might teach next month, if not next Monday — but since I see whole language as a philosophy rather than a collection of things to do, I generally resist offering teaching activities. I prefer to share stories about classroom events and student growth. Most of my own experience had been with primary students, however, and I literally had no stories to share with this audience. So I faced a real problem, which led to the decision to develop a thematic unit on robots — a decision born partly out of my interest in the potential impact of robot technology upon society and upon our concept of what it means to be human, partly out of sheer desperation.

I enlisted Joel's help, and our journey of discovery began. In November we started gathering and developing materials for a whole language unit that would foster reading, writing, oral language and thinking while the students explored interests and concepts dealing with the impact of robot technology upon society. We planned to develop sample lesson plans together, but first Joel would prepare a bibliography of children's literature and films dealing with robots and I would locate suitable non-fiction books and prepare reading-strategy lessons, plus activities that might be valuable in introducing major themes.

Being something of a science fiction buff, I couldn't stay away from narrative literature altogether. I reread the title story from Bradbury's *I Sing the Body Electric!* and read Nostlinger's *Konrad,* noting passages that might be useful for encouraging children to describe and write about a robot member of their own family. I also delved into *Machines That Think: The Best Science Fiction Stories about Robots and Computers* (Asimov, Warren and Greenberg). This marvelous collection confirmed what Joel had suggested about robot stories: that literature embodies not only our fascination with robot technology, but also our fears about it, including the fear that somehow robots will rob us of our distinctive human identity. This fear, I concluded, would be one of the major concepts to be explored in the unit.

Pressured by Joel, I roughed out other concepts that might be explored as well, all linked by a general premise something like this: Robots will increasingly have both positive and negative effects upon individuals and society, as well as upon our sense of ourselves as human beings.

The actual classroom activities, I thought, should emerge from a meshing of these predetermined concepts with the interests the students expressed during their exploration of the topic. Together, the variety of activities would involve virtually all aspects of the curriculum. I conceptualized this meshing as follows:

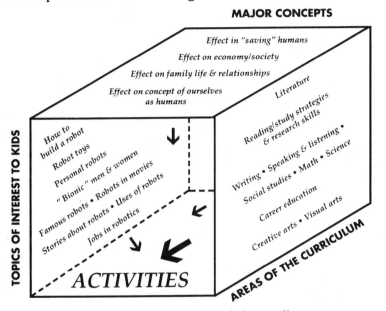

MAJOR CONCEPTS

Effect in "saving" humans

Effect on economy/society

Effect on family life & relationships

Effect on concept of ourselves as humans

Literature

Reading/study strategies & research skills

Writing • Speaking & listening •

Social studies • Math • Science

Career education

Creative arts • Visual arts

AREAS OF THE CURRICULUM

TOPICS OF INTEREST TO KIDS

How to build a robot

Robot toys

Personal robots

"Bionic" men & women

Famous robots • Robots in movies • Uses of robots

Stories about robots • Jobs in robotics

ACTIVITIES

By this time I was convinced that calling my presentation "A Whole Language Unit on Robots" was a contradiction in terms. Nothing so prepackaged could legitimately be termed "whole language." Maybe it would be better to call it "Developing a Thematic Unit on Robots" and to emphasize how teachers might develop a thematic unit *with the children*. We soon abandoned the idea of preparing sample lesson plans, since it was clearly incompatible with our growing recognition that such a unit should be developed jointly by teachers and students.

Nevertheless, I continued to work on "introductory" activities. I became personally fascinated with much of the information I found and with the questions my reading raised for me. (Did you know that there are already self-replicating robots that have the potential for colonizing the moon or another planet? I didn't until I read Karen Liptak's *Robotics Basics,* a book appropriate for students in the upper elementary and middle school/junior high grades.) In the hope of getting students as excited about robots as I had become, I prepared an "anticipation guide" for discussion. I knew this would need to be simplified for younger students, but it was a start.

Anticipation guide

According to your prior knowledge, decide which of the following statements about robots are true (T) or likely (L), and which are false (F) or unlikely (U).

1. Robots have computers for brains.
2. Robot messenger carts deliver papers and packages in many large offices.
3. Some robots can "see," some can "hear," some can "feel."
4. Someday, you may be able to hire a robot to babysit while you go out for the evening.
5. Robots were used to explore the sunken ship *Titanic.*
6. Robots could become more intelligent than humans.
7. Some robots can learn things for themselves.
8. Robot means "worker."
9. Some factories are run almost entirely by robots.
10. The first walking robot was built before 1900.
11. One kind of robot can read books to the blind.
12. Some robots can "reproduce" themselves.
13. Someday, robots may have brains that are made of human protein rather than electrical circuitry.
14. Robots have performed scientific experiments on Mars.
15. A robot spacecraft has been sent on a mission to a star over 10,000 earth years away.
16. Robots have beat human chess champions at chess.
17. Some robots have been designed to negotiate with terrorists.
18. There really are "bionic" men and women.
19. Some robots respond to a human voice.
20. Robots may someday develop emotions.

Answers to or information bearing on most of these questions can be found in Karen Liptak's *Robotics Basics* and Joyce Milton's *Here Come the Robots.*

I also prepared several activities that could be used after the anticipation guide to introduce children to topics and concepts they might like to explore:

~ Patricia Lauber's *Get Ready for Robots!* might prove useful for involving children in designing their own personal robot/mechanical servant.

~ Excerpts from *Konrad* or from *I Sing the Body Electric!* might encourage children to design and write about a robot family member or friend, one with whom they would have an emotional attachment.

~ The "Blue Collar Robots" ad from Joyce Milton's *Here Come the Robots* should arouse interest in exploring how robots might affect workers and the economy.

~ Recalling famous robots from stories and movies, such as C3PO and R2D2 of *Star Wars* fame, would likely stimulate a general interest in robots, and the robot quiz from Milton's *Here Come the Robots* might help to expand that interest.

~ My fictional "news" account of robots taking over Los Angeles (written after I'd learned about self-replicating robots) might stimulate writing, dramatization and discussion.

~ A summary of an article in the July, 1988, issue of *Science Impact* on "neural network" computers might involve the children in a consideration of what makes humans unique. (Those computers aren't programmed to give predetermined responses, but rather to make increasingly more accurate and appropriate decisions on the basis of "experience" — much as a human being learns.)

Each introductory activity I devised would introduce one or more of the major concepts or topics I thought we might consider, and conversely, each of these concepts or topics would be introduced by one or more activities. From there, the students could explore whatever they found most interesting. Individually and/or in groups, they would choose what books to read, what projects to undertake, and how to share what they were learning — with the guidance and assistance of the teacher(s), of course.

Joel and I fully intended to develop the unit in one or more elementary/middle school classrooms before the Winnipeg conference in February. But by then Christmas was approaching and it was too late to do more than put the finishing touches on the materials we had prepared. Somehow I would have to make do with our 16-page handout, plus the six-page bibliography. So in February, swallowing my panic and guilt, I flew to Winnipeg.

The Winnipeg experience

I still have vivid memories of that conference. It gave me my first sight of cars plugged into electric outlets in parking lots. It allowed me to meet some wonderful people and hear some inspiring talks. But mainly it provided me with a significant opportunity for personal and professional growth. As I later wrote in a thank-you note to Orysia Hull: "Spending those few days with you and others at the conference was a 'peak' experience for me."

But of course, growth rarely comes easily. In this case it was preceded by the aforementioned panic and guilt and accompanied by some embarrassment.

Those three uncomfortable emotions began vying with each other during lunch the day before I was to present my session. Someone mentioned that she had been attending an exciting session on "theme cycles" presented by Bess Altwerger from Towson State University in Baltimore. Theme cycles? My luncheon companion sketched Altwerger's distinction between theme *units* and theme *cycles*. A theme unit, she said, was *teacher-oriented*, with the topic predetermined and the teacher responsible for planning and organizing, based on his or her learning goals. In contrast, Altwerger conceptualized theme cycles as *student-oriented*, with the topic negotiated and students and teacher sharing responsibility, based on the knowledge, interests and questions both could contribute. I nearly choked on the *hors d'oeuvres.* Obviously what Joel and I had developed was all too close to what Altwerger was describing as a theme unit. Just as obviously, a "real" whole language teacher would develop a theme cycle, in the classroom, with kids.

And what a "real" whole language teacher would do mattered because this was a whole language conference and I was supposed to be modeling whole language teaching.

That night I prepared a transparency based on Altwerger's distinction. The next morning, after attempting to interest the participants in my anticipation guide on robots, I turned to this new transparency and explained how I thought our unit on robots was somewhat more holistic and child-centered than Altwerger's concept of theme units, but still significantly short of the ideal represented by her concept of theme cycles.

All of a sudden the room came alive with questions and comments. The participants weren't much interested in robots, but they were intensely interested in larger issues. They asked questions such as: "As a teacher, how do you reconcile the school-determined curriculum with the whole language principle that the curriculum should develop from the interests and needs of the children and teacher?" Thinking fast, I suggested that after lunch we should arrange our chairs in a circle and explore these issues, forgetting about robots.

The afternoon discussion turned out to be one of the most exciting I have ever participated in. I did little more than ask each person to state what questions he or she most wanted to have addressed, and then sit back and listen as the group responded. Towards the end, a man who finally identified himself as a school trustee observed: "You know, you people aren't just talking about 'whole language.' You're talking about 'whole life.'" Precisely. Whole language *is* whole life.

And thanks in part to the accolades of people like Chalmers Means, Orin Cochrane and Peter Krause, for one shining moment I felt like a "real" whole language teacher/learner. Why? I can think of four reasons:

~ The conversation proceeded according to *our* agenda. It developed jointly, not according to any predetermined agenda of my own.

~ We were using language for "real" purposes that mattered to us.

~ We were genuinely interested in learning from each other and contributing to each others' learning.

~ The learning outcomes were not predetermined, but developed during the process of discussion.

The sharing of our uncertainties and fears, our uncomfortable compromises and contradictions, became an empowering force. Some of us returned home to make significant changes in our teaching strategies. Others, strangers until then, have since embarked on joint ventures that we hope will have a positive impact on our profession.

What an intriguing paradox: that by admitting to our weaknesses, we gain strength!

Challenge to discovery

I returned home excited by new realizations and new resolve, by new friendships and new opportunities. But I still had to deal with the robot albatross and the promise I had made to Joel that our joint work would result in something publishable.

More reluctantly than Joel may have realized, I suggested that we submit an outline for a book tentatively titled "Developing Thematic Units: A Whole Language Approach" to Adrian Peetoom at Scholastic Canada. But I was privately determined that we would develop such units *with kids* before publishing anything.

Adrian must have read my mind. When he called, he said he was interested in our idea but thought that what would be most helpful was a "teacher/researcher" sort of book, with classroom teachers reflecting on their experiences in exploring a theme, and us participating in, observing and reflecting on the process. "You know," he said, "what empowers teachers is hearing and reading about others' experiences. Document your pain, your growth, what you've learned about yourselves as teachers." Hmmm. An exciting challenge, I thought.

And so this project began.

Joel ~ What is whole language, anyway?

I was intrigued when Connie asked me to help find materials for her presentation on "Science, Technology and Literature." She was thinking about using "factories and automation" as a springboard for discussion, but was having a hard time finding relevant children's books. As an untenured assistant professor I was eager to help, provided something publishable grew out of it.

Standing in front of the public library in Kalamazoo, Michigan, we came up with what seemed like a better topic: "robots." We still aren't sure who first suggested the idea, but whoever it was, we both thought we had struck pay dirt. Robots, after all, were "in." They were popular in such movies as *Robocop, Blade Runner* and *Star Wars,* and in TV shows like *Small Wonder, Star Trek: The Next Generation* and *Conrad.* Transformers (robots disguised as cars, trucks and airplanes) filled the toy stores. And a quick trip back into the library revealed more children's book titles on the topic than we could ever hope to use. Moreover, a robot topic was closely related to Connie's original interest in automation.

Connie explained that her presentation would have a "whole language" emphasis. What she didn't know was that I wasn't really sure what she meant by "whole language," let alone whether or not I was a whole language teacher — or wanted to be one. I had a vague sense that whole language meant getting rid of basal readers and teaching reading and writing across the curriculum, and that it was relevant to no one but the reading teachers who had invented it. *I* would be interested in the literary aspects of the project, I concluded, and leave the whole language stuff to Connie.

As I began working with her, however, I found myself becoming more and more interested in what Connie had to say about whole language. I, too, believed that students should help create their own curriculum, choosing the books they would read and the topics they would write about. Secretly, somewhat grudgingly, I began reading a few books on the subject. What I read was interesting, though sometimes vague.

As I struggled to define the concept for myself, I discovered that many of my colleagues in children's literature were criticizing whole language adherents for using children's books *only* to help children learn how to read, with little concern for literary quality or personal response — one book on dinosaurs or mummies was as good as any other. Later Connie convinced me that while this kind of abuse of literature can be found among teachers eager to "do" whole language without really understanding it, the whole language approach in fact emphasizes the enjoyment and appreciation of quality literature. But at the time I shared my colleagues' doubts.

I was still convinced that whole language was more a kind of curriculum than a philosophy when I began teaching a course in writing for elementary teachers. But I had always believed in teaching writing as a process and, as I read and reread books by Donald Graves, Lucy Calkins and Donald Murray, some of what I had read earlier about whole language also began to make sense. I loved the writing workshops described in Lucy Calkins' *The Art of Teaching Writing,* despite the fact that she seemed to discourage specific writing assignments.

In search of Toad's list

As Connie flew off to Canada armed with materials on robots, including the lengthy bibliography I had produced, I began reflecting on my own experiences both as a college teacher and as a sixth- and seventh-grade teacher in a middle school. Maybe, without even knowing it, I had been trying to be a whole language teacher for a long time.

My reading had convinced me that in practice whole language involved at least three things:

1. *Whole language teachers give their students choices, including freedom to negotiate their own curriculum. Students aren't locked into reading only certain texts or writing on the teacher's favorite topic.*

This was something I had always appreciated as a student. I still remember an Introduction to Shakespeare course at the University of Utah in which a professor let us vote the first day on which plays we would read. At the time it seemed very revolutionary — I was shocked to think that I might have something to say about my own education. In fact, were it not for professors who let their students create their own curriculum, I would never have become a professor of children's literature. When I was a graduate student, we had few formal opportunities to study children's literature, so I redesigned a number of literature seminars for myself by focusing on children's books in the papers I wrote. (My professors would probably be surprised to find themselves described as whole language practitioners, but in many ways they were.)

I tried to give my students choices, too. As a middle-school teacher, I allowed the children to respond to literature in a variety of ways, choosing some of the texts they would read and writing about personal experiences and topics that mattered to them. When I taught freshman composition, my students chose the topics of their research papers, usually focusing on something related to their major field. I have received student papers on Ted Kennedy and Chappaquidick, MacIntosh and IBM computers, funeral homes, wheat bread, *Dynasty,* skiing and vampires.

Now my children's literature students read books they choose themselves and develop annotated bibliographies of children's books on subjects of personal interest. In a graduate course on the young adult novel, my students had a number of options for their final project, depending on their own interests. They could create lesson plans, analyze young adult films, compare young adult and adult texts, or create thematic groupings of young adult novels.

2.   *Whole language teachers try to make what they teach real and relevant (to use the old '60s cliché).*

"Real" books, significant writing assignments, interdisciplinary studies — these are tools that help make learning important to the individual. Thematic units can also be useful, provided they're not canned, prepackaged materials, but more like theme cycles (see pages 12-13).

A focus on theme has always been an important part of my teaching, largely because of an English methods course I took as an undergraduate in which NCTE's *Thematic Units in the Teaching of English* had been one of the class texts. While I wouldn't advocate following any unit rigidly, that book helped me see the value of thematic study. I remember that one unit focused on the future and included a computer program for writing poetry. One focused on death, another on folk traditions. Such units provide students with a context for their studies, stimulating interest in both reading and writing — if the students care at all about the unit's theme to begin with.

During that methods course I designed two units much like the NCTE models. One drew heavily on Studs Terkel's *Working,* a collection of interviews with people about their jobs. Another used Harper Lee's *To Kill a Mockingbird* as the focal point of a unit on prejudice. I was very proud of my ingenuity in creating these lesson plans. (I must admit they are still in my filing cabinet, although I've never taught either one).

When I became a fulltime middle-school teacher, I dutifully tried to use thematic units with my classes. I taught a unit on medieval times, one on *The Adventures of Tom Sawyer,* and one on prejudice and families, based on

Gail Rock's *The House Without a Christmas Tree* and Barbara Robinson's *The Best Christmas Pageant Ever*. They were largely teacher-directed, but I always provided my students with some choice. The response activities were undertaken by groups working on different projects: illustrating and creating covers for books, writing and presenting plays and dramatic readings, composing songs based on literature, building castles, reading more books, writing thematically related poems and sequels to books they had read, etc. It seemed that I was most successful when the students chose what they wanted to do themselves.

3.   *Whole language teachers promote literacy by providing students with positive, enjoyable experiences with literature and writing.*

This is something I have always considered important, as does Katherine Paterson, two-time winner of the Newbery Prize. In *Gates of Excellence: On Reading and Writing Books for Children,* she makes a good case for helping children find pleasure in their books:

> *In all the furor about the right to read and basic education, there is often, it seems to me, something missing. Why are we so determined to teach our children to read? So they can read road signs? Of course. Make out a job application? Of course. Figure out the destination of the bus so that they can get to work? Yes, of course. But don't we want for them the life and growth and refreshment that only the full richness of language can give? And when I say this I am saying with Joan Didion that we fail our children if all we give them are the platitudes, the clichés, the slogans of society, which we throw out whole to keep from having to think or feel deeply.*
>
> *We cannot give them what we do not have. We cannot share what we do not care for deeply ourselves. If we prescribe books as medicine, our children have a perfect right to refuse the nasty-tasting spoon. (p.17)*

Of course, there is no way to ensure that our students think or feel deeply. As a beginning teacher, I secretly wished I could find the magic formula or list of ideas that would make sure they did. I suppose I was a lot like one of my favorite fictional characters, Arnold Lobel's Toad. In the first story in *Frog and Toad Together,* Toad makes a list of everything he has to do during the day. Unfortunately the list blows away and he can't chase after it because doing that isn't on the list of things he's supposed to do. As a new teacher, I wanted a list telling me everything I needed to do to be a perfect teacher. Meticulous planning and rigid thematic units were the closest thing to such a list. Sometimes I relied too heavily on such plans, not allowing my students to pursue ideas not on my list.

Today if I made a list of things I believe would help turn students into Katherine Paterson's kind of reader, it would include the following things:

~ teaching reading across the curriculum;
~ making a variety of reading materials available;
~ using reading discussion groups;
~ reading aloud.

This last activity (teacher-centered as it may seem) was and still is an important part of my teaching. It also saved my life for the first couple of years I taught. Many of my sixth- and seventh-graders came from families that didn't promote literacy. There were few magazines and books in their homes; they had the lowest reading and language arts scores in the district. Some of them couldn't read anything at all. So reading aloud became a part of my daily teaching routine.

In fact, the best memories I have of my two years at West Jordan Middle School are of responses to read-alouds:

~ a boy falling off his chair because he was laughing so hard at a scene in Wilson Rawls' *Summer of the Monkeys;*
~ a whole class of low readers groaning because the bell interrupted the climax of Mollie Hunter's *A Stranger Came Ashore;*
~ two students who could barely read transforming Gail Rock's *The House Without a Christmas Tree* into a play;
~ two other students creating and, dressed in period costumes, presenting something like an early rap version of Mark Twain's *Tom Sawyer.*

Is whole language possible?

My struggle to define whole language continued, and so did my self doubts. Maybe I wasn't a whole language teacher after all. For one thing, despite my good intentions, I always felt a need to control my classroom. In what Connie calls my "rage for order," I planned my classes for the entire semester or year. Relinquishing control to students was very difficult. Like Lobel's Toad, I was not very flexible.

I began to wonder if whole language was possible in a "real" classroom. In my first teaching job I had taught the "core" class for a group of sixth-graders. Theoretically the students stayed together for language arts, reading and social studies during a three-hour block, and I could integrate the teaching of these three subjects. But in practice that was nearly impossible. First, there were constant interruptions for assemblies and announcements over the PA. I was also locked into teaching each subject at specific times because some of the students were pulled out for "resource" language arts and remedial reading, so I didn't have all the students for the whole block of time. Moreover, the district imposed a strict set of objectives, effectively stifling any creative tying together of the three subjects:

I was further frustrated because the unofficial chair of the language arts program was very territorial. We were not to spend a great deal of time on dictionary use, for example, because the eighth grade had a dictionary unit and we might "spoil things" for them. He also believed that the main purpose of language arts was to teach grammar, especially diagramming sentences, a practice my professors had convinced me had disappeared from the face of the earth!

I wondered if I was worthy of the whole language "order." It seemed a little like joining a monastery; only "the chosen" were real whole language teachers. My pre-service students felt the same.

I remember one wintry day sitting on the tenth floor of Sprau Tower on campus staring out at a rather bleak Kalamazoo landscape as one of my former students complained about his student teaching experience. He was determined to go out into the world and preach whole language, and I had always been certain he would become a fine teacher. He was struggling, however, because his cooperating teacher didn't believe in creative drama, writing workshops or reading from trade books. He described her as "traditional." She taught one subject at a time, slavishly using basals and textbooks, then moved on. Did he dare to "cross" her by doing something else? After all, he needed a good report from her for his teaching file.

Other students wondered how they could possibly take time in a very full day to have children write for an hour or more. What would the parents say if they threw out the basal reader or eliminated spelling tests? In my classes they related writing, literature and reading, but they often felt those plans would be the "exception." Could they invest that much energy every day when they taught in the public schools?

Connie's Winnipeg experience raised even more questions for me, particularly as she and I prepared for another conference. We presented our materials on robots to a polite but somewhat subdued audience. What they seemed to want was a full-blown unit they could teach with little work of their own. They wanted Toad's list. But supplying such a list or unit would, we knew, be going against the very principles we were teaching our students.

As Connie and I continued to work together, we found ourselves planning a book on "Whole Language and Thematic Units." We even signed a contract, although we had very little idea what the book would include. Perhaps that's the proper way for a book on whole language to develop, without a list like Toad's that says what we can and cannot do.

We realized that if we were to practice what we were preaching to our students, we needed to explore a theme *with teachers and students*. I think I was a little less apprehensive about this than Connie was. Since I had taught themes before, I somewhat smugly assumed that what we were trying to accomplish would be easy. In the meantime, I privately decided that this project would be my test case for whole language. Somehow or other I would figure out what it was and whether or not I could legitimately be admitted to the ranks of whole language teacher.

And so this project began.

Scott ~ One teacher's journey

While we were driving home after a long evening of running errands, my daughter slumped next to me in the front seat. Suddenly she sat bolt upright and exclaimed, "Daddy, look. That tree is bare naked." Nestled in the midst of a grove rich with fall colors stood a single tree with nary a leaf on its thick, gnarled limbs. With one sharp, vivid response, my four-year-old daughter had captured the scene perfectly.

My daughter's outburst had a profound influence on my life, for it started me pondering questions I had pushed to the bottom recesses of my mind. One question in particular challenged my beliefs and my role as teacher: if children react so powerfully and vividly to the world around them, how can we play upon their natural curiosity and spontaneity to bring these rich, emotional responses into our classrooms? It started me on a journey that has added deep satisfaction and profound joy to the routine pressures and frustrations of teaching in a public school.

Using the basal

For many years I asked my students to check their emotions at the door. Drawing upon their lives and feelings simply didn't fit into the teaching style prevalent in my school. Our language program was built around a basal series. It was beautifully packaged, with lavishly illustrated stories taken from real children's books, and with skills lessons and a teacher's manual so detailed that a teacher could run the program with very little thinking or effort.

Every conceivable question was answered somewhere between the covers of the manual: which skills to address, when they should be taught, what questions to ask during discussions, what vocabulary to practice, what to test, and on and on. To set the reading machine in motion, all anyone needed to know was how to read the teacher's manual and how to run the copier. But spontaneity, creativity and the strong force of life that courses through all children wasn't apparent in that magical guide.

It would be difficult to overestimate the influence of that basal on our reading program. It colored every aspect of language learning and squeezed the life right out of the children.

By their nature, basal programs do that. First, they are standard-manufacture, teacher-driven vehicles. Every idea, every activity, every story comes from the manual. Nothing arises from the students' own interests or needs. Students have no input into the reading process, and thus no personal emotion vested in reading. The natural interest in reading they may carry to school with them is squeezed out by the teacher-controlled reading program. There is simply no room in the front seat for students.

Secondly, basals provide little time to read. The emphasis is on skills, skills and more skills. In our particular program, only one or perhaps two days out of a week's unit were set aside for reading and discussing stories. The other days were spent teaching skills in isolation, followed by hours of dittos and workbooks to reinforce the skills taught in the reading groups.

Two things bothered me about this approach. First, with so little time spent reading anything other than the vocabulary-controlled basal reader, my students had little opportunity to put the skills into practice while reading real literature. They could do the skills in the isolated and controlled environment of a workbook page, but there was little transference of specific skills to meaningful reading situations. Despite completing workbook after workbook and passing one criterion-referenced test after another, my students were not becoming more fluent or discriminating readers. They just plodded along from one imposed objective to another.

Secondly, putting workbooks and dittos at the core of the curriculum holds up a horrible model for children. Workbook writing is invariably dull and flavorless, without the slightest literary value. To paraphrase Jane Hansen, what we do to keep students busy in school shows them what's important to us. By requiring page after page of workbook reading, I was telling my students that reading carries the pain of boredom along with it, and will add little pleasure or texture to their lives.

On the face of it, the basal reader itself countered the negative model of the workbooks. It was attractively packaged and filled with stories by such famous children's authors as E.B. White, Judy Blume and Roald Dahl. But despite its big-name authors and beautiful illustrations, it failed to excite the students much more than the workbook did.

They spent little time actually reading and discussing those stories. Much of the "reading" time was spent drilling skills, introducing vocabulary, and otherwise preparing to read the selections. More importantly, the stories were often watered-down versions of the originals. The writing of Blume, Dahl, White and company was edited to fit the space and vocabulary requirements of the basal, and in many cases only a bland semblance of their style and rich language remained.

My basalized classroom

Classrooms in which basal readers are used have a certain look and feel to them. If you had walked into my room on a typical day, you would have seen something like this:

~ The room is so quiet that the hum of the fluorescent lights is the loudest noise in it. Perhaps you have to look twice before noticing the students sitting in desks arranged in neat rows, churning out answers on worksheets for their neat seatwork folders. It's impressive how well they stay on task and how efficiently they move from one assignment to another. They never leave their seats except occasionally to sharpen a pencil.

~ The only adult-size chair in the room is behind my desk. This desk is the command post of the entire operation, continuously cluttered with folders, manuals, papers to correct, and stacks of dittos needed for seatwork assignments. In fact, it's notorious for its clutter. Somewhere is a sign a colleague once gave me: "If a cluttered desk signifies a cluttered mind, pray tell what does an empty desk signify?"

~ Behind the desk and along the walls are low shelves filled with teacher's manuals, a few professional magazines, and worksheets run off for the week's seatwork. As the year progresses, those shelves will fill up with worksheets, like drifts of snow filling the hollows of an open field, pushing anything but the most essential objects right off the shelves.

~ In the corner, a reading group is in progress. A handful of students are sitting around a table with me, pointer in hand, drilling them on the word-attack skills to be covered that day. Or perhaps I'm leading a discussion on a story from the basal reader, with the teacher's manual in my lap.

~ Three display boards hang on the walls, covered with neat, commercially prepared decorations. If it's close to a holiday, it's likely that a cut-and-paste art project is taped to the concrete walls, the paper faded by the afternoon sun.

My room was also defined by two things that weren't there. One of those was the sound of voices sharing ideas — an unusual and unnatural situation since by their very nature schools are social places. I took people the same age who shared many of the same interests, placed them in a confined area, set them with elbow touching elbow, and then spent much of my time and energy suppressing their desire to talk! Instead of using the social context of the classroom to foster collaborative learning, I rubbed and chafed against the grain by keeping my students chained to their chairs with their mouths locked closed.

There was also a noticeable lack of children's writing on the walls. Basal language programs have children spend a great deal of time decoding print, but virtually no time producing it. As a result, my walls were decorated with posters, charts, bulletin board displays and an occasional art project, but with no children's writing — no words generated by the students to communicate their ideas and bring the fresh breath of their lives into the classroom.

There is a certain amount of irony in this. As a teacher, I was in the "word business." One of my goals was to get my students to use words to create meaning and to better understand the world around them. Yet there was little observable evidence from the classroom that I took this goal seriously. Few original student publications graced my walls. As Frank Smith suggested in *Insult to Intelligence,* if visitors from a distant galaxy had landed on earth and visited my classroom, they would have had to conclude that our written language is merely a "decoration, an alternative to wall paper." In fact, in my classroom it was rarely even a decoration; in no way would anyone have seen it as a vital means of communication.

In short, my program was like many across the nation: smoothly functioning, efficient, flowing from one reading skill to another. My days were routinely the same, joined together seamlessly, with hardly a bump to distinguish one from another. But, while my routine was efficient, it also sucked any fresh ideas and spontaneity right out of the room.

Tip-toeing on the edge of whole language

Then, slowly, some chinks began to appear in the wall of routine. One cold November evening I attended a workshop that presented a simple, clear, easy-to-implement writing program. The very next day my students began to write regularly, and the whisper of fresh ideas began to blow through the classroom. I read the works of Lucy Calkins, Donald Graves and Donald Murray and began to follow some of their suggestions. Along with the children's writing came the life and spontaneity I found so lacking in the basal reader. The whisper of fresh air in my classroom became a gust.

My curriculum supervisor encouraged me to try using trade books in place of the basal reader, and I began with books like *Stuart Little* (E.B. White), *Bridge to Terabithia* (Katherine Paterson) and *My Side of the Mountain* (Jean Craighead George). No more would we plod through watered-down versions of classic stories; we would go straight to the source.

Switching to real children's literature dramatically changed the atmosphere in my classroom. Instead of giving dull, unresponsive answers to canned questions from the basal, my students became more emotionally involved in class discussions. They began to respond more strongly to the books, to live and breathe along with the characters they were reading about, and to form strong opinions about the issues the stories raised. Our discussions began to crackle with intensity as the students watched between the lines for the deeper meanings of what they were reading. Instead of word-decoders they were becoming meaning-makers.

My own job changed as well. Before, I would spend my evenings correcting the mounds of paper generated by the basal-driven system and creating dittos to reinforce the skills taught in the series. When I threw the basal reader out of the classroom, the workbooks went out as well. Now I spent my evenings immersing myself in the delightful world of children's literature, searching for books to share with my students. I spent a great deal of time thinking of questions and assignments that would tap my students' higher-level thinking. I wanted them, as Madeline L'Engle put it, "to dig beneath the words" and into the minds of the characters they were reading about.

I searched for ways to teach skills in the context of the children's own reading and writing. I studied the current professional literature, looking for ways to hook my students emotionally into the books we were studying. My job changed from paper-shuffler to the much more fulfilling role of creator of my own materials. Switching to a new method of teaching created a sense of renewal, and as a result, my enthusiasm for teaching matched step-for-step the excitement my new methods were creating in my students.

The core literature approach

I had arrived at what one researcher, Zarrillo, has identified as the "core literature" approach: I was using particular pieces of children's literature as the basis, or core, for teaching reading. I bought trade books in classroom sets, one for each student, and based discussions and learning activities on that piece of core literature.

This approach has many advantages. First, children abandon the artificial, tepid prose of the basal reader and enter the realm of real children's literature. This fact alone raises the instructional level in the classroom. Children are more likely to emotionally "buy into" a well-written, finely crafted book like *Stuart Little* than into the cramped, limited style of the basal. Discussions become more interesting and sparks begin to fly.

Second, the core literature approach replaces the skills-in-isolation emphasis of the basal with a strong emphasis on comprehension. Assignments become more meaningful, designed to tap into the higher-level, creative thinking of the students. For example, the reading-writing connection is exploited more fully.

Finally, a strong piece of children's literature coupled with an open, inquiring classroom environment creates a heady brew of words and ideas that foster a wonderful attitude towards reading.

Core literature, then, was a solid step in the right direction. It allowed me to do many things that I couldn't do within the framework of the basal program. It allowed me to saturate my students with words — words from the books they read in class and from the stories they were creating on their own. Together we were creating what Nancie Atwell has called "a literate environment," where true literacy takes precedence over the passing of criterion-referenced tests.

However, the core literature approach has one characteristic that limits its effectiveness as a teaching tool. Like its basal counterpart, it is very much a teacher-driven vehicle. All activities, no matter how creative or thought-provoking, come directly from the teacher's mind. There are few opportunities for the students to work their own interests into the process of learning. Even the core title is selected by the teacher. No matter how well-written the book, there will be some students who resist its lure. It simply won't match their interests or needs at that particular time.

The core literature approach is a bigger, fancier model, but in many ways it's the same teacher-driven vehicle as the basal. It is certainly more pleasurable to ride in, but the students' place is still firmly in the back seat.

Moving into theme exploration

At this point, a vague uneasiness began to form in the back of my mind, and a stale feeling began to creep into my classroom. I felt I had taken the core literature approach as far as I could, and that I needed to open things up so the students had more say in the curriculum. I was ready to climb another step of the ladder of whole language.

It was then that I heard about Connie Weaver's desire to do some classroom research involving theme exploration. I read her proposal carefully. Impressed with her plan to allow children to negotiate their own projects within the framework of a general theme, I quickly responded to the opportunity to get involved.

And so this project began.

Whole language principles as goals

The observation is sometimes made that there are as many definitions of whole language as there are whole language educators. But there is widespread agreement that certain principles are crucial to a whole language philosophy of learning and teaching, and we wanted to reflect those in our work on this project — in fact, they became our goals. We'll briefly describe some of them here, in four overlapping categories and with illustrative anecdotes, and again in outline form in Appendix 1, pages 207-212. In the two retrospect chapters (pages 118 and 159), we'll consider how they were actualized, in differing degrees, within our individual and collective experiences in our theme exploration projects.

Of course, our experiences did not reflect all of these whole language principles equally. We didn't all have the same goals, nor were we always or equally conscious of implementing them in our day-to-day planning and our moment-to-moment teaching. Nevertheless, they offered a rough guide for our decision-making and have provided a solid basis for reflection and future growth. Perhaps that is the best any of us can expect.

Learning and the learner

This category encompasses both what is (or should be) learned and how it is learned. We hear repeated calls for "back to the basics," a cry that often translates into phonics drill (reading), handwriting practice (writing), and memorizing the multiplication tables (arithmetic). Recently we've heard demands from people like E.D. Hirsch that students be taught the names, dates, places and events that characterize the cultural heritage of the Western world.

Whole language educators certainly agree that the development of skills and the acquisition of factual information is important. However, they tend to emphasize broader kinds of learning, such as developing the ability to engage in complex mental processes like reading and composing, and developing an understanding of the concepts and relationships without which the accumulation of factual knowledge is no more than an exercise in trivial pursuits.

Facts can be memorized fairly easily (and forgotten just as readily), but complex processes can be mastered and concepts developed only gradually, by actively engaging in the processes, and by actively transacting with the external world and with other people.

The research giving rise to this perspective is varied and complex. It includes the work of genetic epistemologist Jean Piaget, Russian psychologist Lev Vygotsky, educator/ philosopher John Dewey, literary theorist Louise Rosenblatt, humanistic psychologists Abraham Maslow and Carl Rogers, linguist Michael Halliday, literacy educators and theorists Don Holdaway and Brian Cambourne, Frank Smith, Kenneth and Yetta Goodman, Donald Graves and Lucy Calkins, Carole Edelsky and Karen Smith, to name just a few.

Many of the principles that characterize whole language are included in the work of these people and others (see pages 195-206 of the bibliography). For instance:

1. Significant and enduring learning is constructed by the learner, not imposed from without. Such learning is *transactional*. That is, the learners construct meaning for themselves by actively transacting (interacting) with other people, with books and other printed matter, and with objects and materials in the external world.

~ ~ ~ ~ ~ ~ ~ ~ ~ ~ ~ ~ ~ ~ ~ ~ ~

Scott ~ Natural learning

I once had a student who was not particularly strong in school science. He struggled with "paper and pencil" and traditional "book learning" assignments. Yet he did quite well with the hands-on experiments we did, and in one area he was head and shoulders above his classmates: he had an uncanny ability to estimate distances and weights in metric. During a Mini-Metric Olympics (a series of competitive events that tests students' metric skills in an Olympic-like format), he did exceptionally well. His estimates were only a few centimeters off the actual measurements. In other words, he could apply abstract book information with adult-like precision.

One day I happened to run into this student's mother in the office. By way of small talk I mentioned her son's incredible ability to estimate distances and weights. She wasn't surprised. Her husband had a profound love of carpentry and woodworking, she told him. As soon as the son could toddle, he had followed his father to his workshop. Together they would hammer and saw, emerging hours later with some kind of homemade project.

Because these projects were important to the boy, his measuring and estimating skills were honed to a fine edge over the years. In a warm, loving, natural environment the father had taught his son a special skill in a way that is rarely matched in school. The father modeled behavior, praised improvement, increased the level of difficulty as his son became more capable, and provided relevant hands-on experiences that allowed the boy to apply some rather difficult concepts. The result was a child who, despite having to struggle in so many areas of formal schooling, could estimate and measure far beyond the fourth-grade level.

~ ~ ~ ~ ~ ~ ~ ~ ~ ~ ~ ~ ~ ~ ~ ~ ~

2. Learning that is perceived as *functional to* and *purposeful for* the learner is most likely to endure. That is, learning lasts longer when it results from something that arouses the interest, meets the needs, and furthers the purposes of the learner in the here-and-now.

3.   In order to engage themselves wholeheartedly in learning, learners must be confident that they will be safe from negative repercussions. That is, the environment for learning must reward risk, not punish it.

~ ~ ~ ~ ~ ~ ~ ~ ~ ~ ~ ~ ~ ~ ~

Joel ~ Book reports

Towards the end of elementary school I really became excited about reading. I liked books, stories, magazines — anything I could get my hands on. Of course, as in many schools, we had to prove we had read something by writing book reports. After several weeks of reading, I turned in a number of book reports and, to my dismay, my teacher told me that I couldn't have written them: they were "too good." I must have copied them from reviews, or my parents had helped me. (This same teacher told me I was lying when I finished reading assignments before anyone else.)

I was devastated — accused of cheating and, indirectly, judged to be "dumb." That night I told my parents what had happened and returned to school the next day with a note supporting my contention that I had written my own reports. My teacher quickly tried to smooth things over, but I didn't get an "A" in reading, nor was I chosen as part of the group of "good writers" to help create the play our class produced at the end of the year.

Fortunately, in junior high I encountered two teachers who encouraged me and who gave me confidence to continue both reading and writing. As a teacher myself, I've always tried to be careful about the feedback I give my students, and resist the temptation to judge my students' abilities too quickly.

~ ~ ~ ~ ~ ~ ~ ~ ~ ~ ~ ~ ~ ~ ~

4.   If learning opportunities are authentic and risk-rewarding, learners will naturally *engage* themselves emotionally and intellectually in experiences that generate learning.

5.   Although there are developmental trends among learners, learning is fundamentally idiosyncratic, even chaotic. That is, the nature and course of each individual's learning is *unique*.

6. Individual learning is promoted by social *collaboration:* by opportunities to work with others, to brainstorm, to share, to try out ideas and get feedback, to obtain assistance. That is, learning is facilitated when the classroom is genuinely a community of learners.

Summary

Significant and enduring learning occurs most readily when confident learners, supported by the teacher and each other in a risk-free environment, grow and develop in their own way and at their own pace through actively engaging in authentic learning experiences that are functional and purposeful for the learners.

Nature and development of the curriculum

These principles of learning have important implications for curriculum:

1. Since learning proceeds best when students engage in authentic literacy and learning experiences, the curriculum should not consist of worksheets and dittos but of *opportunities* to engage in the myriad kinds of natural reading, writing, discussion, experimentation and research that children and adults voluntarily do outside of school. "Opportunities" also implies an element of *choice* for learners.

~ ~ ~ ~ ~ ~ ~ ~ ~ ~ ~ ~ ~ ~ ~ ~

Joel ~ I hated social studies!

When I was in sixth grade I hated social studies. And it wasn't entirely the teacher's fault. That year we were studying world history and geography, and if there was one thing my teacher knew about it was world geography. She showed us slides of the trip she had taken to Africa the year before and pictures from earlier adventures in Europe. The classroom even had a bulletin board with the caption "Around the World in 180 Days," which was approximately the length of the school year.

I hated social studies, however, because most of the time was spent completing worksheets that could be answered by merely consulting our textbook. We didn't even have to read the book, just look for the words that were in bold face and copy their definitions. It wasn't until I discovered historical novels like Elizabeth George Speare's *The Witch of Blackbird Pond* and *The Bronze Bow* and Marguerite de Angeli's *The Door in the Wall* that I realized that history was about real people, children like me.

That year I won the library reading contest and received a copy of the most recent Newbery Prize winner, *I, Juan de Pareja* by Elizabeth de Treviño, a fictional autobiography about a black slave in 17th-century Spain. It taught me more about history than anything I learned in class. It was only then, when social studies became significant to me, that I began to take an interest in what school could teach me about it.

~ ~ ~ ~ ~ ~ ~ ~ ~ ~ ~ ~ ~ ~ ~ ~

2. Since choice is an important factor in learning, the curriculum is in many respects *negotiated among the teacher and the students.* And since a negotiated curriculum is most often built around topics and themes of particular interest to the students, both language and literacy develop through and across the curriculum. Ultimately the teacher determines in what respects and in what instances the learners can make choices, but many curricular decisions are made by the teacher and students together, both during long-range planning and in the daily give-and-take of the classroom. Such decisions take into account the students' interests, the requirements of the externally imposed curriculum, available resources and so forth.

~ ~ ~ ~ ~ ~ ~ ~ ~ ~ ~ ~ ~ ~ ~ ~

Joel ~ Chelsea and the penguins

In third grade, my daughter Chelsea became fascinated with penguins. Following the gift of a stuffed-toy penguin, she decided to collect penguins (she now has thirteen). She also began to watch for books on penguins. Marilyn Kleine, her teacher, suggested that she read Richard and Florence

Atwater's *Mr. Popper's Penguins,* which she did read several times. That one book wasn't enough, so I found her a couple of others: *Little Penguin's Tale* (Wood) and *Tacky the Penguin* (Lester). I blithely assumed that she would soon grow out of her interest and didn't think much more about it.

Chelsea had never been very interested in writing reports, until her teacher encouraged her to go to the library on her own and (not in connection with any classroom assignment) to find out more about real penguins. Soon Chelsea was reading informational books such as *Animal World: The Penguin* (Rourke Enterprises), and describing to our family the varieties of penguins, their nesting habits, the food they eat, etc. All on her own she wrote a report about penguins and read it to her class. She didn't receive extra credit for writing it, but that wasn't the point. The teacher very wisely let her pursue an area of great personal interest, which engaged her in more intense reading and writing than the usual school assignments did.

~ ~ ~ ~ ~ ~ ~ ~ ~ ~ ~ ~ ~ ~ ~

3. Since learning opportunities need to be perceived as functional and purposeful for the learner, it follows that language itself must be kept *natural and whole.* Emergent readers will be helped to read rhymes, songs and repetitive and predictable stories rather than the stilted, unnatural language known as "basalese." They will read picture books and other authentic works of literary quality rather than the contextless bits and pieces of language that characterize worksheets and workbooks. Also, they will write authentic stories, poems, letters and other pieces, not assignments like writing a story called "The day I woke up as a pencil," copying a poem from the chalkboard, or filling in the blanks on a workbook page.

4. Direct and indirect instruction concerning the *parts* of language will occur in the context of the *whole,* and in the context of the students' needs. For example, the teacher will show one or more students how to punctuate dialogue when those students have actually written dialogue in a story, rather than through an

isolated lesson on quotation marks. Phonics skills will be developed through writing, and in the context of enjoying rhymes and songs, for example, rather than through worksheet practice. Skills are taught not only in the context of the whole, but as the need for them becomes apparent in the course of engaging in some authentic learning experience. The need for the skill is inherent in the task the learner is trying to accomplish, so the focus moves from whole to part and back to whole.

~ ~ ~ ~ ~ ~ ~ ~ ~ ~ ~ ~ ~ ~ ~ ~ ~

Connie ~ Skills in context

John's first-grade teacher wanted her students to learn their address and telephone number, in case they got lost. She wrote each child's address and phone number on a piece of paper and asked the children to practice by copying the information ten times. John devised an efficient copying system: he copied each letter and number ten times in columns. Of course he didn't learn anything about his address or phone number.

Shortly afterwards he wanted to play "repair man" at home with his little carpenter's kit. When I pointed out that a repair man needs to record the name, address and telephone number of each customer who calls for help, John began writing this information down every time I "called" to have him repair something. At first I needed to dictate the information, but soon he had learned both his address and his phone number.

~ ~ ~ ~ ~ ~ ~ ~ ~ ~ ~ ~ ~ ~ ~ ~ ~

5.   Direct teaching does not follow a predetermined scope and sequence chart, but occurs in direct response to the students' interests and needs, to their actions and comments, and to the teacher's observations. For the teacher, each of these is a "teachable moment."

Summary

In whole language classrooms, teachers and learners negotiate significant aspects of the curriculum, students engage in the authentic kinds of learning experiences that characterize people's lives out of school, and direct teaching of skills occurs primarily within the context of these whole learning experiences and the students' interests and needs.

Teacher roles in facilitating learning

Whole language principles of learning, as well as the characteristics of curriculum and teacher roles, draw heavily on research into the early acquisition of language and literacy. For this reason, what has been observed to facilitate language and literacy acquisition in the home has implications for the learning environment in school. In the professional bibliography, pages 195-206, we have indicated a number of reasonably accessible references describing that research.

In acquiring our native language, what we learn are not simply words and phrases, but also *elements* and *rules*. There are rules of various sorts, three major kinds being phonological (sound), morphophonological (meaning/ sound), and syntactic (grammar). Toddlers, for example, learn a sophisticated morphophonological rule when they learn how to form the past tense of regular verbs: add a /t/ sound if the verb ends in an unvoiced consonant; otherwise add a /d/ sound, or /id/ if the verb ends in /t/ or /d/. We know children have learned this rule when they abandon "I went" for the regularized "I goed," or discard "Mommy bought it" for "Mommy buyed it." Older children learn rules like the following for sequencing adjectives: adjectives of number precede adjectives of age, which in turn precede adjectives of nationality, as in "the four young French girls" (Hartwell, p. 111).

Of course, these and many other rules that govern the production of English sounds, words and sentences are not rules the children learn consciously. Indeed, most adults don't know them consciously and may find them hard to understand, much less to remember or teach to someone else. Yet their speech is governed by them, and direct instruction plays no part in the learning of them.

What do parents do to facilitate their children's acquisition of language and the rules that characterize it?

~ They model, or "demonstrate," adult language structure and how meanings can be mapped onto words by talking with and in front of their children. They may simplify sentence structure and vocabulary, and focus on the here-and-now, but they usually speak in natural language patterns.

~ They illustrate (demonstrate) a variety of language functions incidentally, by using language for various purposes as they interact with their growing children.

~ They expect success and demonstrate that expectation consistently, allowing their children to grow into language at their own rate.

~ They respond positively to their children's efforts to communicate, focusing on content and intent rather than on the form or correctness of the utterance.

~ They respond positively to their children's efforts to use and control language, rewarding successive approximations of adult language rather than demanding correctness prematurely. The children receive enthusiastic response for what they can do, rather than repeated criticism for what they can't do yet.

Many children even learn to read in the home, in much the same natural way as they learned to understand and speak the language. In those cases the parents usually:

~ read to their children, demonstrating what it is to be a reader;

~ illustrate the symbolic nature of printed language by pointing out such features as words that stand for people and objects in the pictures, and sometimes running their finger under those words to demonstrate the link between spoken and written language;

~ reread the story upon demand;

~ encourage their children's efforts to retell the story by reading the pictures and reconstructing the meaning;

~ discuss the book with their children and respond to their children's questions (What does that say? What sound does that make?);

~ exude pride as their children's efforts to read the book become increasingly tied to the words on the page.

Often the parents don't recognize that the children are teaching themselves to read. But when whole language educators talk about the "natural" acquisition of literacy, they are referring to the means that parents have used, more or less naturally, to foster their preschoolers' development of literacy. Whole language teachers foster literacy in the same natural way:

1. They are *role models*. In order to foster their students' development of literacy and learning, teachers must *demonstrate* that they are themselves passionate readers, writers and learners. They also need to demonstrate what it means to be a *risk-taker* and a *decision-maker*.

2. They are responsible for creating a *supportive community of learners* in which everyone (including the teacher) is free to take risks without fear of negative consequences, and in which everyone is supported by others. Within this community, teachers encourage *collaboration* in various ways and forms.

~ ~ ~ ~ ~ ~ ~ ~ ~ ~ ~ ~ ~ ~ ~ ~

Scott ~ Learning from peers

Each year our school puts on a music program for the local community. The shows tend to be elaborate and complex, with scores of kids having parts of some kind during the production. Merely getting kids on stage at the right time takes a lot of practice and a high degree of student responsibility.

One year, one of the boys could never get on stage quite when he was supposed to. He would miss his cue, leaving the other kids standing awkwardly while he fumbled up the stairs and into his place by the microphone. Each time he missed his cue, we teachers would earnestly lecture him on the necessity of getting where he should be at the right moment. Didn't he understand how crucial it was that the show flow smoothly so we could leave a good impression with the community? He would return to the risers and promptly miss his cue again the next time.

During the final week of practices, after missing his cue for the third consecutive time, the boy returned to his place on the risers. I was about to go over to talk to him when I saw the boy standing next to him lean over and say, "You know, I feel like a fool standing on that stage waiting for you to get up there." Then the girl standing behind him said, "Yeah, you're ruining my part too." Soon a small chorus of whispers poured down on the boy's head. The comments were neither mean nor threatening, but the other students informed him in no uncertain words how they felt about his irresponsibility.

From that point on, through the last practices, the dress rehearsal and the final production, the boy didn't once miss his cue. What the full power and authority of his teachers couldn't manage, his peers accomplished with a few well-chosen comments.

~ ~ ~ ~ ~ ~ ~ ~ ~ ~ ~ ~ ~ ~ ~ ~

3. They are also *facilitators*. For example, they offer students learning experiences and choices, help them consider and acquire the resources needed for their projects, and guide them in learning valuable strategies and skills for carrying out their purposes. Often, they serve as a mentor, a master to whom the students are apprenticed, and from whom they learn such crafts as reading and writing. They respond to their students' needs, whether articulated or merely observed.

4. They treat students as capable and developing, not as incapable or deficient. They *respond positively* to what the students can do, while *issuing invitations* and *offering challenges* to stimulate their growth.

5. They *collaborate and share responsibility* for curricular decision-making with their students, thus encouraging

them to take ownership of and responsibility for their own learning. By encouraging decision-making and risk-taking without fear of negative consequences, teachers *empower* students to become independent, self-motivated learners and doers.

Summary

Whole language teachers facilitate learning by demonstrating what it means to be a literate person and a learner; by creating a supportive learning community; by serving as mentors, facilitators and collaborators; by responding positively to their students' work and offering them invitations and challenges; by sharing responsibility for the curriculum with their students and encouraging them to take ownership of their own learning; and by encouraging risk-taking and decision-making, thus empowering their students to become lifelong learners.

Assessment and evaluation

In whole language classrooms, assessment and evaluation reflect many of these principles of learning and teaching. In the professional bibliography on pages 195-206 we have included a number of resources that help to clarify the nature of assessment in whole language classrooms and provide concrete suggestions for assessing student progress. Some of the points they make are:

1. Evaluation is based upon *numerous assessments of various kinds,* not upon a single assessment such as the score on a standardized test. Recorded observations constitute the backbone of whole language assessment, but various other means are also used, including periodic performance samples (of writing or reading, for example), data from conferences and interviews, inventories and questionnaires, dialogue journals and learning logs, and student-kept records.

2. Assessment is *ongoing and continuous,* intertwined with learning and teaching. As students engage daily in a variety of learning experiences, teachers make observations about their progress, then use those observations as a basis for making decisions about how to facilitate learning, as well as for evaluation of the students' learning.

3. Assessment data is gathered primarily while the learner is engaged in *authentic literacy and/or learning experiences,* not in a test situation.

4. *Self-evaluation* is an important component of assessment and evaluation. For both student and teacher, self-evaluation provides a basis for decision-making and goal-setting, as does mutual evaluation of the learning experiences in which the students and teacher have engaged.

5. Assessment is primarily *learner-referenced.* That is, the learner's present accomplishments are compared with his or her past accomplishments, more than with external criteria or norms. This practice reflects the conviction that each learner's unique development should be honored.

Summary

In whole lánguage classrooms, assessment is ongoing, continuous, multi-faceted, and based upon the learners' engagement in authentic literacy and learning experiences; observation and self-evaluation are central to assessment; and assessment is, to a significant extent, learner-referenced, emphasizing development and growth as essential to eventual maturity and mastery.

~ ~ ~ ~ ~ ~ ~ ~ ~ ~

The fourth-grade project:
Looking to the future

~ ~ ~ ~ ~ ~

The fourth-grade project began when Connie approached Sharon Otto, principal of Mattawan Elementary School, to find out if one of her teachers might be interested in developing a theme with students in the classroom.

Mattawan is currently the largest elementary school in Michigan, located in a small rural farming community surrounded by upper middle class homes. It has acquired a reputation for being a whole language school. The principal credits school district curriculum supervisor Anne Grandstaff for that, but it's obvious upon meeting Sharon that she has also contributed significantly to the teachers' growth into whole language education.

Sharon and Anne described the project at a staff meeting and then gave interested teachers application forms on which they were to list their qualifications, the reasons for their interest in the project, and so forth. Because Connie wanted to pursue the potentially sophisticated topic of robots, only teachers from the highest grade in the school, fourth grade, were invited to apply. Here is what Scott wrote on his application:

> I have been using trade books as the sole means of teaching reading for the past four or five years.

I am a student of teaching and keep up as best I can on the new research in reading/writing. I try to implement those ideas in my classroom and am extremely open to any new ideas that engage the higher-level, critical reading skills of my students.

I have spent the last ten years working hard to create a "literate" environment in my classroom and developing a strong reading/writing connection. Dr. Weaver's project seems to tie in well with my philosophies and goals. Her project and the goals I try to attain in my classroom seem like "a match made in heaven." Her project and my classroom would fit together like pieces in a puzzle.

And then, at the bottom of the form, Scott wrote "Oh, *please,* please choose me!" Who could resist?

Connie ~ Negotiating the project

To many teachers, the concept of negotiating the curriculum may seem like an unreal, impractical way to teach. It may sound fine in theory and work well in a Utopian society, they say, but it falters in the face of the crushing reality of the classroom and of the world as it exists today.

Yet much of life is negotiated. Few, if any, aspects of our lives are set in stone. Our family roles and responsibilities, our relationships with peers, our jobs and careers — all grow, evolve and change over the years. Negotiation is part of contemporary life, and a necessary life skill that students will put to use long after they leave our classrooms.

Even in its earliest stages, this project demonstrated how real-life agendas are modified as people adjust to each other's expectations and needs. Scott and I began with different ideas about the direction of the project. Following Adrian Peetoom's suggestion, I anticipated adopting the relatively passive role of co-planner and observer/recorder, not teacher. But Scott had different ideas. Here are his thoughts after the first meeting:

Yesterday I met with Dr. Weaver for the first time about the research project we will conduct together next semester. I left the meeting with some apprehension about the project. . . .

Concerning one issue, I have already reached a firm conclusion: I will not be a laboratory specimen being observed by the dispassionate scientist. I think Connie envisions her role as an observer, recording events as they unfold in my classroom. In no way do I want someone planted in the back of my classroom, notebook on her lap, dissecting the things I do.

My primary goal is to grow as a teacher, and that will require a joint and equal partnership right from the beginning. Dr. Weaver's books and ideas are excellent, providing a foundation for many of the principles of whole language. To have someone of this stature in my classroom and not tap into her knowledge would be a crime. The best way to do this is to jump into the project together, with both of us getting our hands dirty. Then we can learn from each other as we muddle through it.

I was equally uncomfortable after our first meeting. When Sharon and Anne kept asking what I wanted to do for the project, I thought: "I just want to sit down with Scott and talk about what we'd like to do, and make decisions together." I was delighted that Scott rescued me from the observer role. I, too, wanted to grow as a teacher, not just document someone else's growth. So we quickly renegotiated the project.

We also negotiated the topic. I wasn't adamant about a robots theme, but I knew it was important that whatever topic we chose should have the potential to raise issues worthy of significant research and discussion. Scott felt that his students didn't know much about robots and therefore might not be interested in the topic right off, or in the economic and social issues involved in the development and expansion of robot technology. "Future worlds" — or perhaps more accurately, what our world might be like in the future — was a broader topic and one his fourth-graders were already concerned about. Will we blow ourselves up?

Will there be clean water and air? What about the ozone layer and the greenhouse effect? Since Scott himself was intensely concerned with such issues, he had already been sharing information and newsworthy items with his class. And that broad topic might easily include learning about robots.

But neither of us seriously considered brainstorming possible topics or themes with the students, then jointly choosing from among those that seemed most promising. We decided to study something that *we* were interested in and already knew something about. Our prior knowledge of different aspects of the topic, and of some of the materials and resources that might be available, provided us with welcome feelings of security as we prepared to undertake a project with so many other unknowns.

Scott's day included a two and one-half hour language arts block in the morning, and we agreed to devote one and a half hours of that to the project every Tuesday and Thursday. As it worked out, however, the power and self-generating momentum of the project eventually made it the dominant theme of the whole language arts block.

This chapter describes our starts and false starts, the routine that developed as we worked with groups of students, the culmination of the group projects and, finally, some of "great ideas" we reluctantly abandoned as demands on our time forced us to make decisions about what was essential and what wasn't. That last section is included to remind teachers that we *all* accomplish less than we may have envisioned, thanks to the day-to-day realities of the classroom and the time-consuming nature of any worthwhile project.

We'll let our journal entries provide you with a sense of what we were thinking, as well as doing, as the project unfolded.

Connie ~ Starts and false starts

Perhaps the most difficult aspect of the theme exploration project was deciding how to introduce it and get it started. Some sense of the inevitable struggle can be gleaned from my early journal entries.

November

Scott and I got together to do some preliminary planning. I had roughed out notes on "the scope of the project." Actually, I'd done a three-part web starting with:

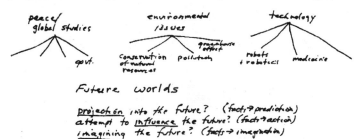

I had also jotted down several subtopics: peace/global studies, environmental issues, everyday life, technology, the nature of humankind. (I kept coming back to my interest in robots!) Scott and I agreed that all but the last topic would probably interest fourth-graders.

We talked a little about how to introduce the overall topic and/or possible subtopics: stories? poems? films? Should we try to get the students involved in a single class project, perhaps with several facets? We also talked about how we might explore the topics: what resources we'd need, and so forth.

We realized that, between us, we have tremendous potential for resources, particularly human, to help us and the kids explore various subtopics of interest. For instance, one of my colleagues is director of the environmental studies program at the university; I have several friends who teach the peace studies course; my friend with the Michigan Department of Transportation can get information on "smart cars" that are being developed, and he might also be able to arrange for us to plant trees on state property somewhere; a friend and former colleague from Iran has written a manuscript for a book on trees, which he hopes is appropriate for about fourth-grade level; another friend sells recycling equipment for Michigan Disposal Recycling; and so forth. Scott has an equally impressive range of contacts. No wonder we decided that the broad "future" topic, with its many potential subtopics, has a lot of possibilities!

As the project developed, we came to realize how fortunate we were to have access to the resources of a fair-sized city and a university community. At the same time, we recognized ever more strongly the wisdom of choosing a topic for which a wide range of community resources is available, whatever those resources might be.

February

I've been wondering since our planning meeting in November how we can introduce the unit. All I can think of are two unsatisfactory alternatives.

We could just say, "Well, kids, today's the day we start our unit on the future" and brainstorm for aspects of the future that interest and/or concern them. That would be a way of going whole-to-part in true whole language fashion, but I question whether that would generate much enthusiasm. [I learned later that Scott had been "priming" them, so that idea might have worked.]

The other alternative is to engage them in several introductory activities that might generate interest, like those I developed to introduce different aspects of robots and robot technology. [See pages 9-12.] We could conceivably do much the same thing for each potential aspect of the entire futures project. However, I don't really like this alternative either. For one thing, it's too much part-to-whole. We could spend several weeks getting the kids ready to decide what they'd like to explore. Furthermore, this approach is highly teacher-directed and ignores the students' prior knowledge. It treats every child as a *tabula rasa,* and that's one thing children are not!

So how can we effect a workable compromise between teacher direction and student direction? How can we generate enthusiasm for moving quickly into the unit? And how will we determine what subtopics to explore?

The first false start

The first idea to become a false start came from me, as the following journal entry describes:

February 19

A possible way of introducing the unit occurred to me last weekend when I stayed overnight with Linda Cameron, an English language arts consultant in Toronto. Linda is a wonderful treasurehouse of ideas for sharing and using picture books with children. We spent much of the evening on her livingroom floor, surrounded by books. She'd say, "Have you seen this one?" and usually I hadn't. But even more exciting were her ideas for improvisational drama, based on some of the books.

On the flight home I remembered a wonderful article by Betty Jane Wagner on introducing a science/social studies unit through improvisational drama. And I began thinking how I might use my fictional "news article" on a robot takeover of Los Angeles to stimulate improvisational drama that, in turn, could introduce the unit.

UPI — Early this morning an army of robots took over the government of Los Angeles, first by taking over their computers and later by bodily taking possession of the municipal building. Government officials and police were powerless to stop them.

The takeover began at 12:01 a.m. when the robots broke computer security codes and gained control of the city's records, as well as its police and security personnel. Within three hours, an estimated 5000 robots had marched on the city. The police, under control of the robots, repelled any citizens who attempted to halt the onslaught. By daylight, the army of robots had taken over all key positions within the city government, including mayor, council, firefighting forces and treasury.

As near as stunned officials can determine, the takeover began five years ago when a firm named Water Everywhere purchased a self-replicating robot from Japan to reproduce robots that would drill for water in the Mojave Desert. Since then the robots have proliferated "like rabbits," as one official of Water Everywhere put it. "But until today they have appeared content to provide water for Southern California and Arizona."

It is not known why the robots decided to take over the city, nor how many other self-replicating robots with similar ambitions might exist elsewhere in the country.

As citizens of Los Angeles, we could brainstorm possible reasons why the robots took over the city. Then, the next day, I could bring in a "news release" from the robots saying they had taken over L.A. because in our typical human irrationality, we humans were on the brink of destroying our society and our planet. This time, we could be the robots and list the various ways in which humans are destroying things. Or half the class could be robots and the other half could be reporters interviewing them, with time for the robots to talk first among themselves about their reasons and for the reporters to decide what questions they'd like to ask.

This was about as far as I had gotten with the plan when Scott called to schedule a meeting. When I shared these ideas with him, he admitted that he had no experience with improvisational drama. He was a little unsure about it, but agreed to try it. We decided to look for some additional ideas and confidence from Larry Swartz's *Dramathemes,* in particular the chapter titled "Tomorrow, Tomorrow!"

As it turned out, we never implemented the idea. After introducing specific aspects of the theme, we concluded that we were adequately launched without spending time with improvisational drama and related activities. I still regret this necessary loss. I think the students would have engaged in some thoughtful and fascinating discussions and writing as a prelude to researching various environmental issues and peace concerns, and perhaps the prospect of more sophisticated robot technology.

A start that came to an untimely end

To introduce the possible subtopic of robots — the topic we thought would most need introduction — we decided to read aloud *Norby, the Mixed-Up Robot,* the first of *The Norby Chronicles* by Janet and Isaac Asimov. We knew that the book was rather sophisticated for students this age, but at the time neither of us could think of or locate any other book for young people that would introduce interesting issues related to robots of the future or other intriguing scientific concepts. (Later we discovered Dean

Marney's *The Computer That Ate My Brother,* an engaging and thought-provoking story more suitable for fourth-graders, but by then the project was well underway.)

Among the questions and concepts we hoped to introduce were:

~ the possibility that robots might develop "emotions";

~ the concept of transmitting matter by changing it into radiation energy that can travel rapidly through space, then back again into matter at its destination — as depicted by the transmitter on *Star Trek*;

~ antigrav devices and travel by hyperdrive;

~ how human life might be different in the future if such concepts were translated into means of travel widely available to the public.

After only two days of reading and discussing *Norby,* however, another book sent us in a different direction. Even so, we feel this brief introduction to sci-fi technology helped to convince some of the students that they wanted to study the technology of the future.

The book that made a difference

At about the same time as we discussed reading *Norby* to the class, we thought of reading *Miss Rumphius* by Barbara Cooney. In it a young girl promises her grandfather not only that she will travel to faraway places and live by the sea, as he has done, but also that she will "do something to make the world more beautiful." Fulfilling her promise, the adult Miss Rumphius sows the seeds of lupine flowers all around her village, generating beauty for everyone to enjoy. At the end of the book, her grandniece, the narrator of the story, makes the same promise, although she also realizes that she doesn't know yet what that might be.

The following journal excerpt describes how we generated discussion from the book, and how we built upon that discussion to get into different subtopics.

February 20

Today I read *Miss Rumphius* to the kids, having them
predict at appropriate points. They understood, intuitively,
that making the world a more beautiful place was a
metaphor for somehow making it a better place. We then
brainstormed for things we could do to make the world
better, and I wrote their suggestions on the chalkboard —
until I ran out of board! These are the suggestions I later
managed to copy (the asterisks indicate which actions the
students thought they could do or affect *now,* even as
children):

~ conserve water: device on faucet to reduce water flow,
  plastic bag with rocks in it to reduce water in toilet tank
  (this one was Scott's suggestion)
~ get rid of greenhouse effect
~ do something about the ozone layer
~ buy safe cars (car with device to keep a drunken driver
  from driving) *
~ stop rape, murder, child abuse, abortion, suicide
~ find a cure for AIDS, cancer, leukemia
~ recycle
~ develop plastic that's recyclable or biodegradable
~ get garbage out of the water (rivers, lakes) *
~ get rid of drugs
~ plant more trees
~ put smoke alarms in homes *
~ have peace instead of violence
~ stop oil spills
~ stop using aerosol cans
~ stop pollution *
~ stop killing animals for furs
~ donate to or join organizations that work toward some
  of these goals *

At this point Scott took over. His own enthusiasm about
Miss Rumphius and its implications got the students worked
up to a high pitch of enthusiasm too. He asked them, "How
did that little seed spread?" and pointed out that Miss
Rumphius didn't just hide the lupine flowers behind a wall.
Building upon the children's responses, he likened Miss
Rumphius's sowing of seeds to throwing a pebble in the
water, creating ripples that spread farther and farther.

Picking up where I had left off, he asked, "How can you stop drugs? How can you be that pebble that spreads ripples?" The kids suggested that they could help friends, not take or buy drugs themselves, start a club.

Next Scott turned their attention to the future which, after all, is the intended focus of the unit. He asked them how, when they grow up, they might help stop child abuse. To reinforce the point, he reminded them of the metaphor of the pebble spreading ripples.

When the students were thoroughly excited about becoming pebbles that spread ripples, Scott invited them to choose one problem they'd like to help solve, do a web showing how to solve it, and then write a paragraph based on the web. Though some of the responses were vague or unrealistic, others were quite detailed, suggesting that the students had already thought deeply about the problem.

Here are some examples:

Making the World a Better Place
by Justin

This is how I could help the world eliminate landfills. Everybody would have to have 5 containers for their garbage. They would have a container for glass, plastic, paper, tin and organic materials. The first 4 you would send to a recycling plant and the last one you put it into a compost pile. To do this we would make bigger, better and more recycling plants. Communities would have to have compost piles for people who didn't have a garden or didn't want a compost pile.

This is how I can: Make the World be a better place
By Maria

I think I know how we can make the world be a better place. I want to try, stop killing animals for fur coats. I think that is really sick. People are killing animals for money and glamour. They

To Make A Better Place!
By: Melissa

To make a better place I'm going to get rid of drugs. When I get older I'm going to make a club where the people are against drugs. We would get a lot of caterpillars and send them to famous and one club. I would put the caterpillars all over coco leaves. We could write a lot of letters to the president asking about drugs.

The End

For many students, this involvement with *Miss Rumphius* may have served to narrow the range of alternatives to consider. Certainly it tended to focus attention on the real, rather than the imagined or the hypothetical. This narrowing of focus was both negative and positive, of course: negative insofar as it tended to shut out other viable options, but positive in that in helped give us, individually and collectively, the necessary sense of direction and purpose for our study.

Getting organized into groups

When we examined the collective list of ideas for improving the world, we concluded that the students' interests fell almost entirely within three categories: *environmental issues, social concerns* and *technology*. To guide a focused discussion of options they might pursue, Scott prepared an overhead showing these three categories, with lines for adding subtopics.

Later he asked the students to indicate their first choice of category on a sheet of paper, giving their reasons. They were to do the same for their second choice as well, and to indicate if there was any group they really did *not* want to work in. As it turned out, their first choices divided them into three nearly equal working groups. I would work with the social concerns group, Scott with the environment and technology groups. We were making significant progress, we felt, although in retrospect it occurs to us that we could have invited the students to group their interests into categories themselves, instead of doing it for them, thus encouraging them to determine the criteria for categorization.

Getting underway

If we were to begin afresh, we would never try to work simultaneously with groups holding such diverse interests. Even with two of us in the classroom, it was impossible to get all three groups started on specific projects at once. Scott had to spend so much time getting the environmental group started that the technology group remained unfocused for several days, and it never did accomplish as much as the other two groups.

Another reason for the difference was that since Scott knew more about and was more interested in environmental issues and the kinds of hands-on experiments they invited, he tended to spend more time with that group. To remedy the situation, we took advantage of volunteer Tom Coder's expressed interest in elementary teaching and invited him to work with the technology group. In the end those students produced uneven but nonetheless substantial progress on their project.

Another problem was the lack of resources. Because the projects required a wide diversity of materials, the resources of the school library proved insufficient, as did those of the Mattawan public library. We ended up locating and bringing in many additional books and articles ourselves, from the Portage and Kalamazoo libraries and other sources within the community.

In retrospect, we feel we should have pursued the topics sequentially, an idea central to Altwerger's concept of theme cycles (see pages 12-13). We wouldn't have needed such a diverse range of resources, and since more students would have been working on the same or closely related projects, more peer consultation and collaboration and less teacher direction would have been possible.

Connie ~ The social concerns group

This group included nine students: Amanda, Brandy, Brian, Jeni, Jenny, Jill, Lisa, Maria and Melissa.

On the very first day of their group work, I encouraged them to consider what they would like to do as a culminating project. The following journal entries show how they came to a decision.

March 17

I wrote down the topics the kids thought they'd like to pursue: child abuse, drug abuse, the homeless and suicide. It was fortunate that I had brought some library books on those topics, since none of the kids had been able to locate any. Then I suggested that we might consider what the group wanted to do as a final project, in order to make our research more focused. Someone immediately suggested a play, and others chimed in with specific suggestions for one! They were off and running without even considering any other possible projects.

Since it was almost time for lunch, I suggested that we all consider other possibilities before the next class. "For example," I said, "we could do a book or a videotape." I really hoped they would choose was a book, because I could envision lots of interesting parts: information on each issue of concern, reviews of books and videotapes, a list of community resources, topic-related personal narratives that we might solicit, creative stories and poems, write-ups of relevant demonstrations. The possibilities seemed endless, and yet I could envision dividing the work in a coherent way.

March 22

We again talked about the nature of the final project. They chose to do a play and videotape it. So much for the best-thought schemes of teachers! Immediately they began talking about props: beer bottles, candy cigarettes, Tic-Tacs for illegal drugs, and so forth. They also began talking about who might play what role, and roughed out some possibilities. In addition, they talked about the sequence of the plot.

I had mixed feelings about deciding so quickly what our culminating project would be. Instead of encouraging the students to read broadly and explore their topic of interest, this quick decision encouraged them to narrow their focus immediately to questions that would be relevant to developing the play. For example, in order to develop the plot and characters effectively, we brainstormed what we might need to know about child abuse: How and why do parents abuse kids? How do kids react, and why? What specific incidents might provide good examples for our play? How do the police handle child abuse? Why do children often not tell anyone they're being abused? On the other hand, this narrowing of focus was necessary if we were to research our topic, write the play, rehearse it and videotape it by the last week of school.

Scott ~ The environment group

This group included Heather, Kristen, Anna, Vanessa, Caryn, Jenny, Kris and Karie. Perhaps an intuitive, unconscious understanding drew these eight personalities together. From the start they were a cohesive, like-minded group. So strong was their thirst for knowledge about the subject they had chosen to study that a kind of glow emanated from them. Here are my notes from the group's second meeting.

March 20

Today I met for the second time with the environment group. After a short brainstorming session and review of our first meeting, I sent them off to a corner to formulate tentative plans about the topic they wanted to study and the form of their final project. At the end of the hour they came back with a clear vision of where they wanted to go and had even elected someone to be their chair-person. Their final project is ambitious but clearly within their ability to achieve.

What they would like to do is break the general topic of the environment into various subtopics: endangered species, air pollution, oil spills (the spill from Exxon's ship *Valdez* was big news at the time), recycling, waste/littering.

In groups of two or three, they will study each subject, write reports and gather experiments. In the end, they would like to share their new knowledge in the form of a science fair type of exhibit displayed in some prominent area of the school or community.

So sure are they of their direction that one girl handed me a list of materials that she needed to conduct her first experiment. They are "rarin' to go."

Scott ~ The technology group

This group was made up of boys: Adam, Jerome, Dustin, Andrew, Robbie, Mike, Steve and Matt. While the environment group spurted ahead, this group's start was much less auspicious. A strong vision or purpose did not emerge for several meetings, and in the meantime the group floundered. Here are my notes from their first meeting.

March 20

The technology group is a different matter altogether. As yet they have no idea in which direction they are going. They have good, even grandiose, ideas — plays, video tapes, a technology museum — but little understanding of the steps needed to get there. After a brief brainstorming session, I turned them loose to discuss the direction of their project and look through the stack of books I had brought in from outside libraries.

The result was a good deal of meandering and drifting. Some walked around the room looking at the papers of other students. Most drew incredible futuristic designs of houses, cars and spaceships. These were flights of imagination, or replicas of things they had seen in movies. They existed only in the students' own minds, with no factual basis to tie them to reality. Meanwhile, the stack of books containing the information the kids would need to mesh their imaginations with current research stood idle.

A routine develops

For two of the three groups, a routine gradually developed once they had settled on their project. One requirement was that each student read a fiction book related to the topic he or she was studying. These were to be read at home, in the classroom during independent reading time, or during project time, if the students didn't have something else to work on. We felt they would gain deeper insight into their topic by combining the affective with the cognitive.

Otherwise, the routines differed from group to group. For now we will simply sketch briefly how the three projects evolved, adding details in chapter five, where we reflect on the concept of negotiating the curriculum and the ways whole language teachers stimulate learning and growth.

Connie ~ The social concerns group

This group researched several topics of interest, wrote a play, rehearsed the play, and finally videotaped it for showing on local TV — although the actual events weren't so neatly sequential. It might seem logical to research the play and then write it, but the students' eagerness to get on with the writing made it more productive to move back and forth between drafting scenes and acquiring sufficient knowledge to develop the characters, plot and dialogue more effectively. Similarly, their excitement about producing the play led them to start acting it out when they had only the roughest sketch of a scene or two. Modifying the "logical" sequence in response to student needs is but one example of what negotiating the curriculum means in actual practice.

The students did their research mainly through videotapes, brochures, speakers and novels, since most of the available information books that discuss such issues as child abuse and drug and alcohol abuse are too sophisticated for fourth-graders. The videos they saw were *It's Okay to Say No to Drugs!* (propagandistic but appropriate for fourth-graders) and selected excerpts from a 1978 NBC special titled *Reading, Writing and Reefer*. Three speakers addressed the entire class: Leonard Marcilous, who described The Ark, a temporary haven for runaways and other teenagers having difficulty coping at home; Judy Milroy, an alcohol and drug therapist; and Mike Hughes, current president of MADD (Mothers Against Drunk Driving), who is permanently disabled and in a wheelchair because of a drunk driver.

Scott ~ The environment group

This group's class time was divided into two general types of sessions. Some days were spent looking through current research and books to find background information about the topics. Using sources such as *50 Simple Things Kids Can Do to Save the Earth* (Earth Works Group) and information I had picked up from the Kalamazoo Nature Center, the students extracted valuable information by "mapping" the material, as suggested by Heimlich and Pittelman. Some of the questions covered in these sessions were:

- ~ What is the ozone layer and how is it being depleted?
- ~ How does acid rain affect the environment?
- ~ What do oil spills do to our oceans?
- ~ What causes the greenhouse effect?

Much of this information was later incorporated into the group's final reports. The following journal entry is fairly typical for this type of session:

April 26

Today we went over some new information that will provide much-needed technical background for their topic. We used *50 Simple Things You Can Do to Save the Earth*. The articles, though written for people older than fourth-graders, worked well with the kids. The book is succinct, straight to the point, and not cluttered with chemical equations and other esoteric scientific references.

I gave the kids markers and had them underline any information that seemed important to them and put question marks by anything they didn't understand. We went through the material paragraph by paragraph, mapping it and drawing pictures and diagrams in the margins, until it became clear to them. They seemed amazed at some of the statistics in the articles. "Six billion tons of carbon dioxide in one year!" was a typical response.

The second type of session was far more interesting to the students. On those days, we tied the information we were finding to hands-on experiments and demonstrations.

There were two reasons for the experiments. First, they would provide excellent displays for our final project. Those who would come to view the project in its final form could share some of the impact the experiments had on the group. Second, the hands-on activities grounded the abstract, "heavy" concepts we were dealing with to concrete situations. This made the material more digestible to the students and also carried an emotional impact not present in the "bookwork" part of the project. It's one thing to read in the newspapers about the oil spill from the Valdez and quite another to feel the oozy stickiness of crude oil on your fingers as you try to clean it out of a bowl of water in the classroom.

The following journal entry describes that experiment, which, along with the students' notes and observations, was one of the central points of the group's final project:

April 20

Had a very interesting meeting with the environment group. We continued our studies of oil spills. We took a clean bowl of water and dumped some crude oil into it. The kids watched the oil fall to the bottom, then bob back to the surface and form a sticky layer of black goo. They quickly deduced that oil is lighter than water and thus floats on the surface.

Their task was to get the oil out of the water. I had brought in various materials — cotton balls, linen, polyester, paper towels and so forth — and had them test which ones best absorbed the oil. They were surprised by how quickly they removed the oil from the water. The black slime disappeared and the water that remained looked clean. But the kids noticed that all was not well. One girl observed, "Mr. Peterson, it's not all out of the water. I can still see floating rainbows."

We set up a long-term experiment in another bowl, into which I once again dumped a jar of crude oil. Except for shaking it now and then to simulate wave action, the girls will leave this bowl alone, simply watching it to see what happens to untreated oil spills. (Wave and wind action causes the oil to clump together, then sink to the bottom, where it disrupts plant and fish life.)

Scott ~ The technology group

The technology group never really fell into a smooth routine. They circled warily around their topic until something grabbed their attention. Then they would burst into a fit of purposeful study until, after a few days, the topic burnt itself out. Sometimes these fits of energy would result in a solid contribution to the final project. Sometimes the students simply chased wild ideas up blind alleys.

Soon the group split into three smaller groups. Adam, Jerome and Dustin took on future transportation as their topic; Andrew and Robbie jumped into air and space travel; Mike, Steve and Matt drifted around the subject of computers.

The main problem was that they didn't really know how to attack the research part of their topic. The books and magazines they were using had lots of pictures that attracted their attention and drew excited "wows" from their lips. Along with the pictures, however, came lots of words in small print. The kids simply did not know how to extract the information they needed from the oceans of ink that lay in front of them.

To get through this log jam, I fell back on techniques I had picked up from whole language books and workshops. I used a combination of the *K-W-L* strategy (What do you already *K*now? What do you *W*ant to know? What did you *L*earn?) and writing-process conferencing techniques to get the group going again. This approach centered their activity and focused their attention on specific questions that needed to be answered. It was highly effective and led the group to a successful completion of their final topic. Compare the following journal entry with that of March 20 on page 59:

March 24

Today as I sat at my desk I was surrounded by kids, some waiting quietly, others impatiently bouncing on the balls of their feet. Some, unable to contain their enthusiasm, broke right into the group I was working with to show me things they had found in their books. Other kids sat around the room, in twos and threes, looking through resource materials.

The mood of the group has changed since our last meeting. On Tuesday the books stood gathering dust in the corner, while the kids drifted aimlessly around the room or doodled spaceships on paper. Today they are beginning to dive into the books to look for answers. What caused the change?

In today's meeting we focused on questions, on things they genuinely want to know about their topic. We listed a few on the board as examples, and then I sent them packing to the corners of the room to further develop their lists. Fifteen minutes later we met as a whole group again and further refined our list.

The computer group, for example, came with these questions:

~ What will computers do in the future?
~ Will we be able to talk to them?
~ Will they have a mind of their own?
~ Will they be able to run our homes?
~ Will they be able to cook?
~ How will Nintendo be used in the future?

Now they're ready to go, with a new purpose to their work. The resource material now has relevance, and they're attacking the small print with vigor.

Culmination of the projects

The products of each group can be described rather simply, leaving for later a more richly textured discussion of selected aspects of the process.

Connie ~ The social concerns group

The play written and produced by the social concerns group was titled "Family Problems." For the full script of the final draft, see Appendix 2, pages 213-221. What follows here is a brief description of the nine scenes:

Scene 1
The scene opens with a distraught mother lamenting that she has lost her job because of her drinking problem. Just as her two daughters arrive home from school accompanied by a friend, the father comes in and immediately accuses the mother of drinking again. Out of their own frustration, both parents yell at the children, who then exit.

Scene 2
The scene opens with the two sisters on the playground at school, talking about how the father hit and bruised one girl on the arm. Two teenage drug dealers approach them, but the girls reject the attempt to sell them drugs.

Scene 3
The girls pack to run away from home. They discuss where they will go and decide to leave a farewell note for their parents.

Scene 4
On the afternoon of the next day the father returns home from work and argues with the mother about her drinking. The mother has found the girls' note and tries to get her husband to focus on finding them, but he is so incensed about her continued drinking that he becomes physically abusive. She breaks loose from his grip and runs for the door. He throws the vodka bottle after her.

Scene 5
A week later, somewhere in the city, the two daughters have run out of money, so they are stealing food from the garbage cans at a restaurant. After successfully running from a man who found them digging in his garbage, they are again approached by the teenage drug dealers. This time the girls accept the proffered joints. The scene ends with them feeling better because of their marijuana high.

Scene 6
Another week later, the daughters are sitting in the park taking turns with a joint and obviously already high. Their friend from scene one comes up to them and tries to persuade them to come home, but they refuse, scolding the friend for meddling in their business. She leaves, crying.

Scene 7
Meanwhile, the girls' mother has decided to try to get help for her alcoholism and for her husband's beating her and the girls. She talks briefly with two alcohol therapists, who assure her they can help. She agrees to return to see them the following day.

Scene 8
Early in the morning the girls' friend again approaches them, just as they are waking up. She tells them she has found a place for them to stay: The Ark. She assures them that they won't be sent home immediately, and that the counselors at The Ark can help them with their drug problem and maybe with their parents. The girls agree to go to The Ark.

Scene 9
After a night at The Ark, the girls return home. The parents are glad to see them, especially the mother. The girls admit they ran away because their father beat them and their mother drank too much. It turns out that the counselors who brought them home are the same ones the mother has been seeing. The play ends with the mother vowing she will overcome her drinking problem and the father finally admitting that he does sometimes abuse the children and could use help. They all agree to work together on their individual and family problems.

We videotaped the play on May 31, and the whole class watched it in July when we had a summer pool party to celebrate the completion of the projects. The videotape was also shown on local cable TV several times the following September.

Scott ~ The environment group

This group's final project took the form of an exhibit mounted on a display board and placed in the main library to be viewed by the entire school. A letter of invitation was sent to the other classes and a "guest book" was left on the table to record the responses of the visitors. It was filled with comments like these (edited for spelling):

I liked that game because it tells people a lot of things about the earth.

I learned what acid rain was and how much money it took to clean the Statue of Liberty.

Troy

I think you should recycle.

I liked reading about recycling.

Julia

I like the part of pollution on the plants and I liked the part of the acid rains. You did a good job.

Allison

I personally liked the frog article. I liked it because I didn't know that they were endangered and I liked the oil part too.

Audrey

You're right. Earth pollution is a problem.

Is the oil drill cost a million dollars?

I learned about that oil sinks down when it turns into a ball.

Here is a brief description of the exhibit:

I. Reports and diagrams

~ Oil spills
~ Eight largest oil spills
~ How oil is produced out of the ocean
~ Diagram of a deep-sea oil well
~ Ozone depletion
~ Diagram of the earth and ozone
~ The greenhouse effect
~ Endangered species (17 hand-drawn pictures of endangered species, with a brief report on each animal)

II. Experiments and demonstrations

~ Oil spills (see page 63 for details)

~ Air pollution: plants
(Two plants were kept under clear glass jars. One was polluted daily with sulphur and carbon from a burnt match. The leaves of the plants were compared to see the effects of polluted air on green plants.)

~ Air pollution: acid rain
(The students carved two identical sculptures out of thick pieces of lime chalk. One of the "statues" was doused daily with a mixture of vinegar and water. The students observed the damage done by the "acid rain.")

~ Air pollution: smoke-stack emissions
(A candle made from animal fat was lit and a tin plate was held over the flame. A black, sooty layer of carbon collected on the plate, illustrating air pollution caused by smoke-stack emissions.)

Descriptions of procedures and observations were written and posted with each experiment.

Scott ~ The technology group

In the end, this group's final project took the same form as that of the environment group. The two displays were exhibited at the same time. Here is a brief description:

I. Transportation

~ Levitation vehicle: a report on a combination car and helicopter
~ Lean machine: a report on a small, light car designed for use in heavy traffic areas
~ Aero car: a report on a car that flies, plus a homemade model
~ Monorail: a report and diagram on the new monorail systems being piloted in Japan

II. Future air travel

~ Fighters of tomorrow: a report on jet fighters of the future
~ Supersonic transport: a report with a diagram and a model

~ S.R.71 Blackbird: a report with diagrams and a model
~ F-16 Fighting Falcon: a report with a picture

III. Computers and robots

~ How a computer works: a report and diagram
~ Personal robots in the future: a report
~ What can robots do now?: a report
~ Walking TV: an illustrated report
~ Virtual world: a report and diagram
~ Robots with brains: an illustrated report

Great ideas abandoned

All too many of our great ideas for enhancing the students' learning had to be abandoned because of pressures of time and circumstance. We want to describe some of them, however, for three reasons:

~ to alleviate other teachers' concerns about not accomplishing everything important;
~ to indicate how we might hope to further stimulate students' learning another year, given more time;
~ to illustrate the potential richness of whole language education.

Students locating their own resources

One of the ways we taught skills in context was to demonstrate how the students might use a bibliography titled *Adventuring with Books* by Mary Jett-Simpson to locate fiction (and some non-fiction) that would be relevant to their topics. Scott did a thorough job of preparing the students to use this bibliography, as indicated in this journal entry by Connie:

March 15

Scott had photocopied the table of contents from *Adventuring with Books* for each child. Using transparencies, he went through it with them, discussing subtopics that might be relevant. As they discussed the topic and subtopic headings and tried to decide which ones might contain annotations for pertinent books, he also mentioned items he thought might interest them. Then he told them to use their own copy to help them locate novels and nonfiction books for themselves. We each left two additional bibliographies of children's books in the classroom for the kids to use.

Scott found that the students returned again and again to the bibliographies on his desk to find books on topics of interest. Why, then, was this extremely successful teaching of "skills in context" abandoned? Because few of the books could be found in the school library, as well stocked as it is, or in the Mattawan public library. So while the students were effectively equipped to use this new research tool, in practice their efforts produced few results.

Outreach journals

The idea of outreach journals, and Scott's preparation for them, can again be documented from Connie's journal:

March 12

Today Scott introduced the idea of an "outreach journal," which he'd heard about at the Michigan Reading Association. This journal combines the two kinds of journals I had originally suggested the students keep: a "response journal" on the novel they were reading, and a "process journal" describing and reflecting upon the processes they were going through in discussing, researching and preparing final projects on their topics.

Again Scott demonstrated excellent teaching strategies. He told the class about the journal, saying that they should include their ideas and reactions to the novels as well as to factual information. Then he emphasized the importance of *detail*.

To get the kids to see the contrast between the relatively undetailed writing people often do and the detailed writing we want them to do in this journal, Scott first asked who had ever been alongside a river. Most of the kids had. He then gave them five minutes to write in their journal everything they saw or would see, hear, feel, maybe smell. The examples the kids later shared were actually rather well done; obviously Scott has emphasized detail before.

He then read them *The River* by David Bellamy, a book particularly appropriate to the concerns of the environmental group. It describes in detail all the animals and insects living on or in the river, detailing also the effects of chemical pollution on the river and river life below a certain manufacturing plant. Scott involved the students in predicting and discussing as much as possible, but the book is long and I noticed that the kids were restless, as when I read them the first chapter of *Norby*.

After the reading and discussion of the book, Scott indicated that we would go outdoors and find a spot on the playground from which to record our sensory perceptions. The kids were eager, no doubt partly because today was a spring day, warm enough for us to go out without coats. Scott told the kids to draw a web, then write a paragraph. The activity went beautifully, as the kids recorded sensory details. Some of us even brought items back to the classroom: animal fur, a chive, a stone. Beginning the sharing, Scott read his own description, drawn from just a part of his web. His detail and use of metaphor were great!

Here are some examples of Scott's descriptions:

I see the sun peeking through a thick layer of gray clouds. My skin tingles from the warmth of the newborn sun.

I feel a gentle wind, heavy with moisture, blow across my face. The wind brings the sweet smell of grass with it.

In the distance, I hear a bird chirping — short, staccato sounds. Another calls sadly, wailing into the wind like a newborn baby.

A tiny ant crawls across my notebook.

At the other side of the playground, the gentle hum of a truck can be heard. A man gets out of the truck and starts a saw — a harsh burst of sound, like a swarm of angry hornets.

On the other side of the pines are the soccer fields. They stand alone, empty, waiting for the soccer season to begin and the thrill of children's feet tickling its back.

I walk over to the pines. The ground is soft and spongy and squeaks as I walk. The fresh smell of pines fills my nose. The tall, skinny trunks of the pines sway softly in the breeze, their needles flowing in the direction of the wind. Pine cones and brown needles litter the aisles between the neat rows of trees.

Again, the trouble with the idea of outreach journals was that we didn't have sufficient class time to devote to writing in them — nor did we remember to encourage the students to write in them outside of class. True, some of the students, mostly those in the environmental group, did use their journals fairly extensively for recording the questions they brainstormed, the materials and procedures they used for experiments, and their general notes. For example:

I feel that this is a good thing for me to do because It's fun and it's interesting. Doing the project is a good Idea I think It will be cool. Studying oil spills makes me feel like I'm figuring out a mystery. For my project I was thinking we could get a bowl and put some water In It and some oil. After we do that we are going to put a nice plant In the water and see how It reacts. Later on we will put some the bowl and see clears up the oil I cleans up the oil It be great but if It work then we know should try to figure another soluteon.

In are group were doing a play. I'm pretty excited. I get to be a conceler. I'm read a book called the Pinballs I like it. I'm on the 8th chapter ifs about 2 bays and one girl. My farvite carictor is the girl One boy gets his legs ran over, by his dads new car. His dad drinks alot to. Yesterday I talk to my family about drugs and what they think about it. I whatheed 21 Jump Street and it was about drugs. My mom and III talked about the show after we whached it. Yesterday I finshed Pinballs. I Loved it! It is now one of my favrite books. Were still working on the play. I think It is going to be great. Today we are going to have a speaker coming in and he is going to talk about drugs I'm going to write down notes.

Many of the students took notes as they listened to the speakers dealing with alcohol abuse, drinking and driving, and the temporary shelter for teenagers. Others commented on the novel they read, as below:

> ❀ ❀   5/4/90
>
> Cracker Jackson
>
> Cracker Jackson is an intresting book, I like it a lot. I think Jackson rite about Billy Ray beating up on Alma. Alma's lieing about the car wrecs. I think rite now Jackson is fibing to Alma that he belives her.
>
>   Jeni

But in general the outreach journals came nowhere close to including the detailed information and responses that we sought. Another great idea that simply faded away for lack of time.

Student-kept records

A third valuable procedure to fall victim to the lack of time was Connie's idea of having the students keep records, during class time, of what they had done in preparation for each class. Such information could logically have been included in the outreach journals, but since her social concerns group was using index cards to record notes about videotapes, they were given index cards to report on their progress also.

> Jill   4/12/90
>
> Books iam reading for child abuse
>
> The child abuse help book
>
>   I cracker Jackson/play

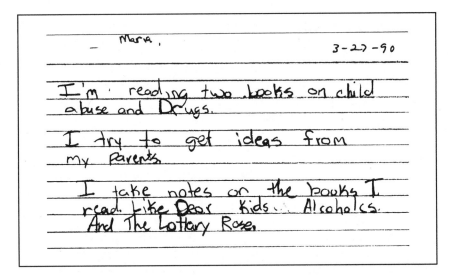

Maria,   3-27-90

I'm reading two books on child
abuse and Drugs.

I try to get ideas from
my parents

I take notes on the books I
read. Like Dear Kids. Alcoholics.
And The Lottery Rose.

This seemed an easy way to amass and file records for determining the extent to which the students were taking responsibility for their own work. Furthermore, Connie reasoned, if the students knew they would be expected to account for their efforts daily in this way, at least some of them might be more likely to read, research and write outside of school.

After engaging in this process twice, however, she again found that she couldn't afford to devote project time to such record-keeping.

Student editing

Once the students in the social concerns group had drafted and revised their play, it would have been logical for Connie to work with them to help them edit their work. In particular, she found many wrong spellings for homophones (like "are" and "our") and she would have liked to teach a mini-lesson on the relevant homophones and then see if, working cooperatively, the students could edit their own work. Again there was insufficient class time even for the mini-lesson, never mind the actual editing. Reluctantly Connie edited the play herself, making some fairly significant revisions in the process.

Literature discussion groups

The activity that Connie most regretted having to abandon was involving the students in literature discussion. One of her journal entries describes the book she unilaterally chose, and her reasons for choosing it. A later entry describes the group's one and only discussion of the novel.

April 10

After our guest speaker Leonard Marcilous left, I barely had time to distribute Betsy Byars' *Cracker Jackson* to my group. Scott had mentioned it as a particularly good novel about physical abuse — in this case, spouse abuse. The protagonist is a boy not much older than my fourth-graders. He gradually becomes aware that his former babysitter, Alma, is being abused by her husband, and he ultimately gets her to go to a facility where she can receive help. The story is filled with humor and sensitivity and is a good read. Besides, it will help my group understand the ambivalence someone feels when being abused by a family member, some of the signs of abuse, and the kind of help available.

This seemed a particularly good choice for my group to read, since I had lined up speakers on the other topics of particular interest but not on child abuse. So I had ordered nine copies from Rollins' bookstore. (I ought to own stock in that place by now!) Anyway, after Leonard left and I had distributed the books, I didn't even have time to suggest that we read a certain chapter or number of pages for next time.

April 17

Today, a week after I first distributed copies of *Cracker Jackson,* we were able to have our first literature group discussion about the first two chapters of the book.

I had brought a new tape recorder to record the session, but it didn't work right. What a disappointment, since the group had a genuine discussion about the book and it was fascinating. I had prepared some questions to ask if necessary, and I did ask some, but I tried to interject them as naturally as possible within the conversation, rather than question the students in the more typical teacher-inquisition mode. Often I would introduce a question with "I wonder."

~ I wonder: What did you think when you read that the envelope containing the anonymous letter was pink with yellow roses? Who did you think it might be from?

~ I wonder: Why do you think anonymous letters are heavier than other letters?

~ I wonder: How did Cracker find out who wrote the anonymous note in school? What did you think about his method? (They thought it was a good method and offered other good ways he might have exposed the note-writer.)

~ I wonder: Why do you suppose the author tells us this? (We generally agreed it was to show how smart Cracker is, how he can solve problems.)

We also discussed things that not everyone seemed to understand, or that different people understood differently, such as why Cracker's dad called him every Thursday, why Cracker's friend Goat and Goat's friends threw wet popcorn over the balcony at the movie theater (did they really mean to hit the girls below?), whether or not Goat actually got out of the house to ride over to Alma's with Cracker, why Goat was phoning Cracker from his bedroom closet.

In several cases we found ourselves rereading the text to decide if we had drawn appropriate inferences — some of us felt the text confirmed our conclusions, some decided to change their conclusions after reading more carefully. It was interesting to note to what extent prior knowledge figured in, too. For example, I'm convinced that Goat was calling Cracker from inside the closet in the hope of keeping his mother from knowing that he was making a phone call. Several of the kids didn't draw this inference, however. Maybe I've made "secret" phone calls before and they haven't? Interesting.

We talked, too, about how Cracker lied to his mother in order to get out of the house and go check on Alma. Some of the kids had read the subsequent chapter in which Cracker explains how his mother worries way too much about little things but not always about big things, like the note from Alma saying that her husband would hurt Cracker if he kept on calling and coming over. (Of course, Cracker's mother hadn't seen the note.) The kids seemed to think Cracker had only done what was necessary in lying about going riding with Goat in order to go to Alma's, and in making a promise he didn't intend to keep. I wanted to ask the kids if they, too, sometimes made promises to their parents that they didn't intend to keep, but somehow we got sidetracked onto something else.

Not surprisingly, the students also related the text to their own lives. Some mentioned family members who have been abused, for example, or incidents in which they themselves have been physically abused by an adult.

All in all, it was a very sophisticated conversation, exemplifying the various kinds of reasoning and response discussed in Eeds and Wells' article "Grand conversations: An exploration of meaning construction in literature study groups." In the process of sharing our reactions, we found we had to deal with literal comprehension and inference, often returning to the text to do so. Also, the students engaged in predicting, analyzing reasons for the characters' actions, hypothesizing about the author's purpose, evaluating a character's actions, and relating the story to their own experiences and their lives.

Connie was eager to continue the discussion next time, and so were several of the students. Unfortunately, they never got back to discussing the book together as planned. The play took precedence.

Summary

B.F. Skinner once said: "Education is what survives when what has been learned has been forgotten." Over and beyond the facts, did the students in this project become "educated" according to Skinner's standards? Did they develop any longlasting attitudes or values beyond the knowledge they acquired from their research? The answer, we feel, is yes, especially against the background of some of Scott's previous experiences.

He had been working for three years on a committee to promote a more secure future through international understanding. The first thing he had done when he was elected to this committee was survey his students to find out the concerns they had about the future. He wanted to find out how they felt about the world they would soon inhabit. From those informal surveys he had discovered three things:

- ~ His students had grave concerns about the state of the world. They were very worried about the possibility of nuclear war, the environment, drug and child abuse, and many other issues.

- ~ They did not have much information about the issues that concerned them. Their sketchy knowledge seemed to come from headlines and snatches of information taken out of context and without the background necessary to put their concerns into perspective. Ignorance may be bliss, but his students' half-formed ideas and vague impressions seemed to exaggerate their fears and concerns.

- ~ The students had few people they could talk with to vent their concerns. Thus, they dealt with their feelings by bottling them up inside, to gnaw silently at the back of their minds.

We think our project did several things to deal with the issues raised by those surveys. First, it gave the participants a sense of empowerment, a feeling that as individuals they could have an impact on the world. Using *Miss Rumphius* as a model, they began to realize that their actions could have an effect on society, that they could "drop a stone into the water" that would ripple out to all areas of the community. The project struck a blow against complacency and self-absorption. It began to develop a sense that individuals can work together to build a better world.

It also demonstrated that the problems that confront our society can be brought from the dark corners of our minds and placed on the table for close examination, to be illuminated by factual information and discussion. The bright light of scrutiny causes our concerns to lose their dark, mysterious qualities, to become less formidable and more manageable. Bringing into the classroom Leonard

Marcilous from The Ark, Judy Milroy as an alcohol and drug therapist, and Mike Hughes from M.A.D.D. exposed the students to competent, caring adults who were already working on the problems they were so concerned about.

The students who took part in the project may forget a lot of things. They may not remember exactly what a C.F.C. is; they may confuse the "greenhouse effect" with the "ozone layer"; they may not remember the exact number of people killed each year as a result of drunk driving. But they will not forget the process they went through to get these facts. They will remember examining issues they cared about with concerned adults; they will retain the attitudes and feelings and values they developed toward difficult issues; they will remember taking steps to better understand their world. We think this process will help them become more caring, responsible adults. In this sense, the students in this project did indeed become "educated" citizens of the future.

~ ~ ~ ~ ~ ~ ~ ~ ~ ~ ~ ~ ~

The first-grade project:
Metaphors and meteorology

~ ~ ~ ~ ~ ~

Joel ~ The search for a whole language classroom

Shortly after Connie and I started planning our theme exploration project, I took a position as an assistant professor of English at Southwest Missouri State University in Springfield. We decided to carry on, however, thinking the move might even help the project. We could try out our ideas in two distinct geographic areas and compare notes. Perhaps we could choose different grade levels.

The move, the second my family had made in two years, was chaotic. Nevertheless, during my first week in Springfield I began to search for a school where I could conduct my part of the project. While Connie found a whole language school with relative ease, my search was more difficult. Since I was new to the area, I knew no local schools or teachers and wasn't sure where to start. As far as I could tell, there were no schools like Mattawan around, with reputations as whole language schools.

Shortly after our arrival in town I discovered the Book Nook, a bookstore specializing in children's and young adult literature. That in itself made me feel good about my move.

On my very first visit I ran into the language arts coordinator of the Springfield Public Schools, a bright woman with a Ph.D. in reading. I immediately told her about our project, begging for her help. She was very polite and seemed interested, but two things she said bothered me. First, everything I did would have to be approved by the superintendent. Second, there were almost no whole language teachers available to work with; Springfield is a "conservative" community.

When my two children started school a few weeks later, I was convinced she was right. Chelsea went into third grade and Brad started kindergarten at an elementary school which, in all fairness, is good in its own way. Chelsea had a difficult time adjusting initially because her previous school had been more flexible and hadn't given letter grades. Here everything was graded and there was little room for error. One wrong answer instantly brought a math paper down to an A–.

Brad's kindergarten class also amazed me. The kindergarten report card had boxes for around 60 different skills that needed to be checked off during the year. Brad never did master "tying shoes," perhaps because his shoes have Velcro snaps instead of laces. He also had a hard time cutting and coloring to his teacher's satisfaction, though he picked up reading very easily. Every day he brought home a paper with the command, "Color more neatly." One of my colleagues had a daughter in that same class who colored *too* neatly; she was so meticulous she sometimes didn't finish her work and had to stay in during recess to finish. On the third day I was told that Brad was "behind," which suggested to me that the other kids must have taken five years of kindergarten preparatory classes.

At back-to-school night I was given a 100-page booklet for each grade, with instructional goals for every subject area. According to these booklets, district teachers were to spend a certain number of minutes each day on each subject. Music, art and library work were separated from regular classroom activity, so it seemed unlikely that I would be able to integrate such things into a language arts lesson in the Springfield schools. Chelsea's teacher, a very kind, nurturing woman, would have loved to work with me, but there was just no time in this system to experiment.

Two things — one serious and one rather silly — finally convinced me to search for a school outside the Springfield school district. First, the teachers did not do much reading aloud. Second, the district did virtually nothing to celebrate Halloween, a children's holiday if ever there was one. It didn't even allow the kids to wear costumes to school or have a party.

So I decided to approach the Greenwood Laboratory School on the university campus. One rainy day I made my way there and had a pleasant talk with the assistant principal, who was very willing to let me work with his teachers. It soon became clear, however, that he had no idea what whole language was, but he assured me that the teachers, who were also faculty members at the university, were excellent. My problem was solved, I thought. But it really wasn't.

The colleague whose daughter was in Brad's kindergarten class pulled her out of public school and enrolled her in Greenwood. He was initially very excited: there were no grades for kindergartners, more field trips and a greater interest in individuals. But he soon learned that things weren't that different. Standardized testing hadn't disappeared. The school, it seemed, wasn't really very flexible, and some of the students were clearly pampered. Moreover, I began to realize that if I had anything to say about whole language I needed to say it in the context of public school experience. I needed to prove to myself that whole language is possible in "regular" schools with "regular" teachers. A laboratory school wasn't "real" to me.

Nora and Vickie

By this time I had begun my own teaching: two classes of children's literature and one of young adult literature. My students were, for the most part, certifying to teach. Early in the semester I discovered Vickie Atkinson, one of those students coveted by college professors everywhere. She was a "non-traditional" student, older than I am. She lived in Conway, Missouri, where she also worked as an aide at Ezard Elementary School in two first-grade classrooms. Each day she traveled to Springfield for her work on a degree in elementary education. She was bright, energetic and an eager learner — and an experienced teacher as well. Besides aiding in the public schools, she had taught music to the children in her church for a number of years.

What really made Vickie stand out in my mind, however, was that she was already a strong believer in whole language. Moreover, she was in a classroom which she believed to be whole language. Time and time again she would talk about Nora Wolf, one of the first-grade teachers she worked with. Nora, it seemed, taught reading to her first-graders using trade books like Ezra Jack Keats's *The Snowy Day,* which I had told my students was superior to books like Margaret Hillert's *The Snow Baby,* a basal-like reader with controlled vocabulary and textbook-type illustrations.

In practice, Nora seemed to have developed a compromise between whole language principles and traditional teaching techniques. She spent the morning teaching the district-mandated curriculum, even using a basal reader. But from twelve until two most afternoons she had a block of "whole language" teaching time. Her students read from trade books, silently and to each other, and wrote frequently. They read to the kindergarten children and to their own classmates in unsupervised groups, helping each other figure out the words they didn't know.

One day I mentioned my project to Vickie and she encouraged me to meet Nora. At first I hesitated. Connie was also going to work in a rural community and I was hoping for something more urban. More importantly, I had no experience teaching first-graders. Other than my university experience, I had taught only in grades six through twelve. I didn't even have an elementary school certificate. If I had wanted to apply for a job teaching first grade, I wouldn't have had the necessary credentials.

There was a selfish side to my reservations as well, since Conway was quite a distance away. Also, I wouldn't be able to do the kinds of writing assignments I might with fourth- or fifth-graders. I was worried. Could whole language work with first-graders who were barely beginning to read and who, in my mind, probably needed a lot of direction?

In the end I decided to talk to Nora anyway, especially since I wasn't sure that whole language was being practiced anywhere in the Ozarks. I have since met a number of area teachers who are trying to grow into whole language, some even in my children's school. Some have been inspired by participation in the Southwest Missouri Writing Project, others through membership in local language arts and reading associations. However, there still aren't very many.

So I found myself driving to Conway to meet with Vickie's famous Nora.

Conway

Conway is a small rural community a little less than an hour's drive east of Springfield, with a population of about 500. I suppose it's typical of many of the smaller farming communities in the area: its claims to fame are a bluegrass festival in the summer and the fact that some famous boxer was killed there. Ezard Elementary School is the only school in town for students from kindergarten through third grade. The school (and the school district) enrolls students from three counties, and thus is large enough for two classes of around 25 children in each grade. These numbers remain fairly stable through high school, where the average graduating class numbers 50-60. Many of the students are bused; a good number live on farms. Most of them come from families without a lot of money. Many come from single-parent homes. When pressed, Vickie admitted that only a few come from families that encourage literacy by providing their children with books or magazines.

I called Nora one afternoon in December and arranged to meet with her after school the following week. She seemed a little nervous about the whole project and clearly felt that I would judge her attempts at whole language as inadequate. The year before had been her first conscious attempt at whole language teaching. Actually, she had long practiced the principles of whole language referred to in chapter three, but to her, whole language meant a particular program.

What was new for her was her attempt to cut back on the use of basal readers and teach her students to read using trade books. In this respect she was an innovator in her school. She was also committed to having her students read to each other and write daily. In fact, when I finally got into the classroom I found that her students were quite experienced in sharing their writing with each other and seemed to like doing it. Nora encouraged inventive spelling and, if her assignments were sometimes more specific than those posited in books like Lucy Calkins' *The Art of Teaching Writing,* she still gave her students a lot of freedom.

The sad part of Nora's experience is that she met with a lot of administrative resistance because of one parent's complaint. She was watched closely and the test scores in her class were monitored to see if her students suffered from her "experimentation." Fortunately, everything seems to have turned out fine.

Upon arriving at the school the first time, I met with Mr. Sweeny, the principal, who was cordial and even excited about the work we were going to do. He admitted that he didn't know a great deal about whole language, but expressed interest in the book Connie was writing for administrators. He was still not a convert to the whole language faith, but he would allow me to work with Nora, no questions asked.

The school itself was much like others I have seen. I glanced at the library. Apparently well stocked. Lots of children on the playground. Bulletin boards. Nothing unusual. When I finally met Nora, I liked her a lot. She was soft spoken, yet firm, and, as I was soon to find out, she had a wonderful ability to communicate with and encourage children. Her classroom looked quite "normal," although I remember noticing the number of books scattered around the room, more than in my own children's classrooms. We talked for a while and I discovered that, while Nora had been teaching for a number of years, she was still experimenting. Because of recent graduate coursework, she was acquainted with many of the current trends in teaching reading and language arts.

At the same time, she clearly wanted me to teach the project more or less on my own. I guess she was hoping to learn from me. Ironically, I was also looking for her to teach me what she knew, particularly since she was the expert on first-graders. Besides, despite Connie's attempts to educate me, I was not especially expert in methods of teaching reading, which seemed important for dealing with her students. Somewhat reluctantly, she finally agreed to do some of the teaching.

In retrospect, I feel that I learned as much from my search for a whole language classroom as from the project itself. For one thing, I realized that the difficulties I had faced as a classroom teacher, difficulties that had made theme exploration nearly impossible, are still present in many classrooms. I also realized that many schools are simply not open to whole language teaching. In the end, the project was shaped by its setting — a classroom in which students and teacher were trying to grow into whole language while forced to adhere to a district-imposed curriculum.

Starts and false starts

On my first visit to Conway I noticed a number of pictures and handwritten stories about robots hanging on the walls of Nora's room. In response to a robot story in their basal reader her students had each created an imaginary robot that could do whatever they wanted. They had then written and drawn pictures about their robots. Some of their "stories" were only a sentence long; some were much more developed. For example:

My Robot plays with
me. We play tag.
But one day we
wint to play tag win
all uf sudn a old
bog kam owe and he didnd
wunt to eat us. he just wanted a
frind. So
from now on he is ore
dog. The End

Jami

ym Robvot will be for
doing work and for fun
em and him I will mace
him do em humwork
and all it hf to do is culr.

Jeff

I like my Robot He
like me to
and my mom too
He can play with me.
The end.

Melissa

I tod the robot to fed
the dog
Wie i was clenen
Mie badrum
When i cam bac
He ax a dentl sta
In the dogs wodor

Brandon

There was obviously a great deal of diversity in the students' abilities. It seemed, however, that this one assignment had nearly exhausted their interest in the subject. I wondered if six-year-olds could really learn much about the complex workings of real robots. Could they build one, as we had envisioned in our ideal lesson plans?

Nora felt that her students were no longer especially interested in that topic. Besides, it occurred to me that the children should have some choice in the matter. We decided that I would observe Nora's students for a week and then teach the following week — with no idea, at the moment, what topic we would be exploring.

The first two visits

My first official visit took place on January 23. Nora and I had decided to wait until things had settled down after Christmas vacation and until my classes had reconvened at the university. Even then, scheduling was difficult. Because of my university schedule, I could visit Conway only on Tuesdays and Thursdays and, with travel time almost an hour each way, for two hours at most. In the middle of that two hours, the students would have a ten-minute recess. On Thursdays, another half hour would be lost for instruction by the school's art teacher, and after that, four or five students would be pulled out of the group for speech and special reading. So I had no guarantee that I could work with the whole class at one particular time. Still, Nora believed in whole language and the students were already used to reading and writing to each other — both big advantages.

We agreed that on my first visits I would stay in the background, observing the students and getting a sense of what was going on in the classroom. At first Nora's class didn't seem unusual: the children completed traditional math worksheets, for example, although she had them play math games as well. However, when reading time rolled around, the classroom came to life. The children all knew what they were supposed to do. Some hurried over to a table filled mostly with trade books. Many had reading books in their desks. They all started reading, excitedly, enthusiastically. Some read in small groups to each other. A few read to Nora. A number came up to me, the strange figure hiding out in the back of the classroom, and vied for the chance to show off their reading competence.

And read they did. I don't know what I expected from first-graders, but I felt this group read quite well — although Nora and Vickie told me that they weren't nearly as good as last year's class. I quite enjoyed the experience. After hearing some of my college students tell me they hated to read, it was refreshing to be with a group that definitely valued reading. It was really amazing. Vickie assured me that, for the most part, these students didn't have books and magazines at home, that their love of reading had been developed in the classroom and nowhere else.

The children were talkative, friendly and fun to be with. One girl asked me if I was the principal because I was wearing a suit, and two others went on and on about my pretty tie. I decided that I should dress somewhat more casually the next time.

I came back on Thursday. This time Nora had them reading and writing. They read a selection from their *My Weekly Reader,* a magazine I had enjoyed when I was younger but had somewhat snobbishly dismissed in recent years as not worthy of children's attention. Nora invited the children to write in response to an ethical question posed in one of the selections: a letter of advice to a character who had found some money. At first I doubted the validity of the assignment, but Nora was excellent at provoking good discussion without being judgmental. What could have become merely a lecture on honesty became a spirited discussion of ethics, without right or wrong answers. (Many of the children opted to keep the money.) The *My Weekly Reader* is written directly to children, and that may be the reason these students liked it. Children intuitively sense when they are the intended audience of what they are reading.

I was not without some knowledge of the age group, with a son in kindergarten and a daughter not long out of first grade. I had, however, forgotten their desire for nurturing and acknowledgement. Several of the children gave me pictures they had drawn. One wanted my phone number. These bids for recognition continued during the rest of the project, and I received a present of some sort nearly every time I visited the classroom.

These early visits were helpful. I began to get a sense of the class itself and the children who filled it. There were incessant talkers, exhibitionists who demanded everyone's attention. There were several children with learning disabilities. One girl had come from India and understood very little English. Another wrote stories that sounded exactly like a basal reader. (Nora sometimes joked with her about that.) Several had speech problems. One boy constantly moved, never sat still.

But one important question remained unanswered: what were we going to do with these students since robots were out? Feeling somewhat sheepish for betraying her trust by junking the robots theme, I called Connie to consult. But she wasn't going to use the robots theme for her part of the project, either — "the future" was going to be her topic, she told me. It sounded great. In fact, I was jealous. She had several wonderful, topical ideas she was going to pursue with her fourth-graders while I was stuck with a group of first-graders. For them, the future was limited to summer vacation and going into second grade.

Connie suggested "flying" as a topic. That might do. Or might it be too technical? Would it work in a classroom that was half whole language and half traditional? What kinds of materials would I use? Another difficulty was that Nora's class spent little time on science study, except for a science fair.

I was also worried about "the E word." How could I empower these students to choose their own curriculum if we imposed a topic on them? It was clear that in a first-grade classroom a theme unit would require a great deal more teacher direction than I had realized. But it seemed important to find a topic that would relate to the children's personal experience.

In the end I decided I would start with something that interested me and see where it went with the students. During the last few years I had been gathering books about weather, especially winter, often using them in my children's literature classes. It seemed to me that this topic would lend itself to personal writing and experimentation. One of the few science courses I had taken in college had been in meteorology, and I was still fascinated by weather. I have since experienced tornadoes in both Michigan and Missouri, and my interest continues to grow.

When I later met Scott, Connie's co-teacher, he suggested that I had chosen a "safe" topic. But I needed a safe topic to begin with. My concern was that regular, "ordinary" teachers needed to be able to apply whole language principles even when they were forced to teach a set curriculum. Weather seemed a good choice, for there were sections on weather in virtually every science book in Nora's room.

After consulting with Nora, I decided that I would teach a lesson on snow and see what that topic might generate. I had visions that circumstances might lead us to a unit on sky-diving or Egyptian pyramids or even storks. I had, after all, read Meindert DeJong's Newbery Award-winning book *The Wheel on the School*. To me, its unnamed teacher was the prototype of the perfect whole language teacher. The students in his small Dutch school had become interested in the storks that once nested on the roofs of their town. In order to bring the storks back, they determined that they would place a large wooden wheel on top of the school, since wheels were often nesting places for these birds. Soon storks and wheels became their curriculum. Maybe the same thing would happen with this group of first-graders; perhaps they would find some unusual topic of intense personal interest which we would all pursue together.

It didn't happen, however, and I'm still not certain that I really provided the students with an opportunity to choose their own topic. They were used to a transmission model of learning, and by introducing the subject of weather I was telling them that I approved of it. Where they could (and did) have a definite impact was in determining what aspects of the subject we would explore and how we would explore them. Since weather itself is such a broad topic, there were many relevant secondary subjects from which the students might choose. The possibilities were almost endless:

- the scientific aspects — weather forecasting, creating weather, understanding how and why weather takes place
- the sociological aspects — how weather affects communities and individuals, how people adapt to certain kinds of weather, how humanity is affecting and changing weather
- the cultural aspects — weather folklore, weather-related entertainment and games, music and art relating to weather, folktales and other stories about weather
- some combination of these

The book that made a difference

The following Tuesday I came prepared to work with Nora's class, though with some trepidation. I began by discussing what the word "weather" might mean. The children generally had a good idea about how weather changes in different seasons, and this gave us a chance to brainstorm some of the different kinds of weather we might eventually discuss.

I then read aloud a story about winter from *Frog and Toad All Year,* in which Frog and Toad go sledding and Toad eventually crashes into a tree. The students responded well to the story — at least they laughed at the appropriate spots.

We talked about winter and snow. I sparked their interest by talking about "pink" and "green" snow, unusual phenomena that occur when bits of rock and plants get mixed with the snow. Before revealing the cause of this strange snow, however, I asked the children to make up reasons why snow might come in such odd colors. The most popular answer was that the clouds had Kool-Aid in them! My information came from a book by Franklyn Branley, *It's Raining Cats and Dogs,* a title the children thought hilarious. I also tried to brainstorm what causes snow, but this didn't go very far. Their simple answer was that God makes it snow.

The children clearly liked the subject matter, so we continued talking about their own experiences with weather. I shared *The Snowy Day,* a simple book in which a young boy engages in fairly typical winter activities: dragging a stick through the snow, making snow angels and trying to preserve a snowball in his pocket. The power in this book is its ability to capture a young child's feelings and experiences.

Nora's class liked the story (some had read it during free reading; most had seen the Weston Woods film). They had obviously felt some personal connection with the book's protagonist, Peter, because they all wanted to talk about their own snowy-day activities. From there the discussion "snowballed." We were soon talking about sledding and snowball fights and making angels. Then we progressed to storms in general. This was even more popular. It hadn't snowed all winter and their snow experiences were sometimes half a lifetime ago, but they all remembered recent thunderstorms.

Eventually we decided to write down our experiences with unusual weather. To help the children get started, I talked about an ice storm and tornado warning I had witnessed in Kalamazoo. The ice storm had made driving impossible, while the tornado warning had forced my family to retreat to the bathroom for safety.

When it came time to write, some of the students wanted a little more direction — freedom was a little scary. In response, I helped them brainstorm some possible topics and ways they might begin to write. Most of the children wrote stories. Some recorded personal experiences; some made up stories about what they would do if they encountered a snowy day. Some wrote only a couple of sentences. One merely made a statement about liking to build snowmen; another wrote a letter to her parents, detailing an occasion when the electricity went out during a snowstorm and the family had to cook in the fireplace. It was clear that they were most interested in themselves, and that would need to be the focus throughout the project.

Here are examples of the writing they produced:

Dear Mr. Chaston

I can ree mebr win me and my
cusns and my ucl had a snuw boll
fite and my ucl hit me in the
chece. frum Jeff

Jeff

Dear Mr. Chaston,

I woold make a
snow Angel if I
went in the snow.

Danielle

I had a cnow bol fit and I
got hit with one and I
kam in and I got now klos
on and kam bkab alt

Jeremy

I lick when it
snows be cus I
lick
to bind snowman

Brandon

I was in a snow storm once.
We was at my G. and G.
when it started to snow but
we didn't now that it would
be a snow storm.

Brandi

Dear Mom and Dad

do you rememdr the
snoow storm the stove
woont wrce we had to
uoos the fore plase
to cook there was a tee
that wos going to fol on my
broths we had to sleep in
the levening room

Rachelle

Both Nora and Vickie also wrote stories, without any
prompting on my part. Since they both adopted the style of
first-graders, using short sentences and specific detail, their
stories became examples of what the children might
accomplish with their own writing. Here is Nora's story:

When I was a little girl the snow came down and the wind
blew so hard that there were high drifts. My daddy went out
with his shovel and dug a snow cabin under the drifts. This
was a fun place to play. It was warm in under the snow, too!
My sisters and brothers and I played inside our snow
playhouse for a long time.

Vickie had also experienced a bad storm and had to cook in the fireplace:

> About three years ago there was a terrible ice storm. We had no electricity for seven days. We cooked in the fireplace. It was fun. We played games and read lots of books. We went to bed early. The trees looked like they were covered with diamonds. We could not watch television, but we listened to the radio. It had batteries. I was glad when the lights came back on.

I was really surprised when the students spontaneously applauded after Vickie and Nora read their stories out loud; it seemed they really enjoyed hearing that their teachers had feelings and experiences similar to theirs.

Clearly we hadn't exhausted the subject. I asked the students if they would like to talk more about the weather and got a resounding *yes!* So we brainstormed again for some of the possible topics for exploration: wind, snow, rain, weather forecasting, tornadoes, and decided that weather would indeed be our subject.

Despite the brainstorming, however, this lesson was very teacher-directed. Even at the time I was uncomfortable with the approach, feeling guilty that I hadn't followed good whole language teaching practices. But the children's reaction to *The Snowy Day,* and their subsequent writing and discussion, signaled something important to me. They were interested in weather (my topic) as long as it related to them personally, but they didn't much care how or why it snows and didn't really want to find out. This didn't mean that we couldn't do some of the weather experiments that were already whizzing around in my head, but our primary consideration would have to be the way weather affects individuals.

A routine develops

Since the students were clearly interested in how weather affected them personally, this was our focus during the next few weeks. As in the fourth-grade project, we gradually began to develop a routine that helped give the project some structure.

Rain and more rain

The Thursday following our discussion about snow, Springfield and Conway were drenched with rain, one of those downpours that produce a couple of inches in one day. If the whole language philosophy were to govern this experiment in theme exploration, it seemed important to make use of the current weather, and I quickly shifted the topic from snow to rain.

Before leaving for Conway I put together a small booklet of rain poems, drawing from books like Beatrice Schenk de Regniers' *Sing a Song of Popcorn: Every Child's Book of Poems,* which has a large section of weather poems illustrated by Marcia Brown; Jack Prelutsky's *The Random House Book of Poetry for Children,* illustrated by Arnold Lobel, and *Read-Aloud Rhymes for the Very Young,* illustrated by Marc Brown.

Ironically, the rain caused my car to stall on the freeway, teaching me only too well how weather can affect a person's life. When I finally arrived at the school, the children were glad to see me. I was drenched and clearly worried about whether or not I would make it back to Springfield, so I spent some time telling them how angry the rain had made me feel. They, too, had definite feelings about the rain. They had gotten quite muddy during recess and would have to stay inside for the rest of the day.

The students were eager to continue with the weather project. A couple of girls gave me paper-airplane valentines they had made in art. One boy later told me that it was "fun" when I came. Since it was art day, I had only a short time with the whole class. However, I had a chance to work with everyone except the students who were with the speech or special reading teachers.

After discussing our feelings, we tried to describe rain.

The children suggested words like *mud, wet, cold, gooshy, boring.* Everyone had ideas. They enjoyed playing with words. We shared Peter Spier's *Rain,* a wordless picture book that depicts the development of a rainstorm and its effect on two children. Like Peter of *The Snowy Day,* the two children play outside in the weather. They fall in puddles, stand in the water as it drains down the sewer, and put their fingers in the rain as it drains out of a water spout. Eventually they go inside and the rain dissipates. Since the book has no words, I suggested that the class create a text. They took turns describing what was happening on each page.

We then read together some of the poems in the booklets I had created. We did choral reading of most of them, with the students following along from their own booklets. Their favorite was one by Rhoda Bacmeister called "Galoshes," and we read that poem several times. The children especially liked its alliteration and rhythm and the way the language sounds like rain when it's read aloud.

After reading the poems, we borrowed words from them to add to our list. The class liked *slooshes* and *sloshes* from this poem, *squelch, squirt* and *squiggle* from Marchette Chute's "Showers" and *squishy-squash* from Polly Chase Boyden's "Mud." I wrote all of these words on the chalkboard — and they quickly corrected me if my handwriting did not match the style of script they were learning!

We decided to write our own descriptions of rain. (I tried to avoid the term "poetry" for the moment.) The children were excited by this project and began making their own lists of rain words and phrases. A few wanted to draw illustrations for their descriptions and others went on to write stories about rain. These were often surprisingly concrete, drawing heavily on the word bank, imitating the poems we had read. The following examples were edited for the class book:

Rainy Days

wet cloudy
mushy
muddy boring
splashy
snowy icy mushy
splashing puddles

Danielle

Rain

I like rainy days.
Wet puddles.
I can jump in them.
Wet and gray.
There are other days,
like snowy days,
but rainy days are my favorite.

Amber

The Rainy Day

When it rains it is slushy
and sloshy and wet and
cold. You can't go outside
because it is rainy. You
can play inside

Jennifer

Showers

Drizzle and drip comes
down with the rain.
Wishes and washes
the cloudy day.

Martha

After that class, Nora and I sat down and tried to do some planning. One obstacle we faced, Nora felt, based on her experience, was that many children in rural Missouri communities are not encouraged to be creative or to ask questions. It might be impossible to turn these first-graders loose without giving them directions. I voiced my concern about the way we were approaching the project. Coming in for only a couple of hours a week seemed a betrayal of the whole language principles we espoused. I wasn't in the classroom long enough to tie weather into other areas of the curriculum, for instance.

Since it appeared that we would have to direct the students through the project, we tentatively mapped out topics for five weeks. We hoped, however, that the students would begin taking more and more responsibility, and we planned two activities that might help ensure this. One was a weather magazine containing the writings the students would do during the project. The second was an empty "big book" made of poster board, which the students would fill with pictures, artwork, etc. The school science fair that would take place in March might also spark some interest.

Because the children often read by themselves, we also felt that creating a classroom library would help them pursue the weather topic on their own. I made several trips to the main branch of the Springfield Public Library and to the Book Nook for books and found more than we could ever hope to use. While much of what I discovered was geared toward older readers, there were a number of useful folktales, stories and poems, as well as informational books, on virtually every aspect of weather.

I added to those my own growing collection of books on weather, and had Nora ransack her school library. Together we produced some 50 different titles. We didn't force these books on the students, just made them available for free reading, along with books on other subjects. But the students frequently gravitated to the weather books, especially those we used with the class as part of the project.

The following Tuesday I played things by ear. I still felt that I was barely beginning to discover what works and what doesn't work in a first-grade classroom. I began another lesson on rain by reading a picture book by Vera Aardema to the class, *Bringing the Rain to Kapiti Plain,* a cumulative poem that explains how an African warrior manages to end a drought by shooting an arrow into the clouds. I asked the children to chant the repeated lines with me as the story progressed, something they clearly enjoyed.

I then asked them if they knew any other ways people have tried to make it rain. They knew about rain dances. One boy claimed knowledge of a special mud ceremony which Native Americans perform to bring rain. Someone else had heard about cloud-seeding, giving me the chance to explain what I had discovered in my own reading. First, I had them guess the number of water droplets in a cloud — there are billions! — and drew a picture on the board to show how raindrops are formed. We then talked about how scientists sometimes "seed" clouds to make it rain.

Following this, we decided we ought to help both the scientists and the people of Kapiti Plain by brainstorming new ways to make it rain. The children were especially partial to throwing people up into the clouds to make holes in them so the rain can come out. One student made this suggestion early on and everyone else wanted to copy him. They got very involved in the discussion, though many of their responses were very silly. I think Nora was a little uncomfortable with the fact that I didn't stress the scientific reasons for rain.

The students were proud of their ideas and some decided to send their suggestions to the people of Kapiti Plain. Others, including Nora and Vickie, wrote stories. As usual, we enjoyed sharing what everyone had written:

Kapiti Plain I wish that you and me can throwe my dog up in the water cloud and macke it rain

Heather

Plece make it rain at Kapiti plain be cuce the anmls will diye then all uf the will diye the end

Joshua

Kapiti plain you nede to Sckream!!!!!!!!

Martha Jean

I will thoe an appel up in the cloud. I hope it will rain cats and dogs

Brandi

Once upon a time the land was very dry because every afternoon the clouds passed right by without dropping any rain. The trees and flowers were so sad and thirsty and dirty that they knew they must think of something to do.

One very old and wise tree had a very good idea. He called all his pland friends together and they worked on a plan. The very next afternoon as the clouds started moving across the sky, every plant started to tell the saddest story they knew. All at once the clouds got so sad that they all started crying at once.

Nora

> Sometimes in the middle of summer when it does not rain for a long time, we sit outside and stare at the clouds. Maybe if I had a big cannon, I could shoot a big cannonball at the clouds. It would make such a large hole that it would have to rain. Then we would have to worry about patching up the hole.
>
> Vickie

One question we didn't have an answer for was how to help the children edit their writing. I remembered Lucy Calkins' discussion of revision in *The Art of Teaching Writing,* where she explains that, for young writers, revision may entail little more than adding on to what has been written, either orally or by stapling a second piece of paper to the first. She also reminds first-grade teachers that even though children don't appear to be listening to one another when they are having peer conferences, "these interactions serve a purpose." (p.61) But both Nora and I were unsure about how to get first-graders to edit their work and how to use peer conferences effectively.

Not only that, we still viewed whole language more as a kind of curriculum than as a set of principles. We were pleased that the children were responding well to the stories we read in class, exploring those aspects of the subject that caught their fancy and writing in a variety of formats. But I was worried that my sessions with the class were beginning to fall into a pattern.

I generally began with a read-aloud of a picture book or poem about a particular kind of weather. I followed that with a class discussion and then a mini-lesson to introduce one form of writing the students might choose to explore in their writing workshop.

I was disturbed because this routine seemed rather mechanical. I wondered if such a structure was providing the children with a chance to explore their own interests, or if we were curtailing their spontaneity and creativity.

Fortunately this particular group of students was spontaneous under almost any circumstances. Nora had already convinced them that they could read and write, and they were used to sharing their ideas and writing in class. Moreover, in my continued reading about whole language and writing instruction I found support for creating a routine within which choice and creativity could be encouraged.

I was quite relieved when I stumbled across chapter six of Jane Hansen's *When Writers Read*. Although directing her comments primarily at writing workshops, she explains:

> *Reading/writing classrooms are tightly structured. They must be. The classroom is full of decision makers, many of whom are inexperienced and need guidelines. To complicate matters, many of us are new at this kind of teaching and don't know how to organize ourselves. We feel certain about only one thing: The classroom must be orderly. (p.49)*

Hansen goes on to say that "a predictable structure provides safety and simplicity," facilitating student response and learning, as well as an orderly classroom. (p.52)

I felt good, also, that virtually all of the students' reading and writing were "authentic literature experiences." The books we read aloud were real books which they could find in the classroom and which they enjoyed reading. And they never wrote paragraphs or sentences; they wrote letters and stories and poems and newspaper articles and instructions.

The water cycle

The following Thursday Nora taught a lesson on the water cycle. She reminded the students of the story I had used in the previous lesson, drawing a stick figure on the board of a man shooting an arrow into a cloud. It seemed clear, after all, that the children knew this wouldn't really make it rain. When Nora asked what makes it rain, they once again responded "God." She finally convinced them to examine *how* God might make it rain. She asked them to consider what happens when they leave water out in a glass for a long time. They already knew it would disappear.

Nora has the ability to elicit responses from her students by pretending that she has a problem or can't figure something out. She brought in a number of books from the library and shared bits and pieces of several of them. She read part of a selection from *Raindrop Stories,* a book about a personified raindrop. The story is no masterpiece, but it does a good job of showing how water goes back up into the air. The class discussed both evaporation and precipitation. Nora then shared bits from *What Makes It Rain?* (Brandt) and *World of Weather* (Adler), which she placed on the chalkboard ledge afterwards. Several children indicated that they wanted to read those books for themselves.

The class spent time looking through magazines and cutting out pictures of plants, trees, lakes and clouds. Nora had taped together two poster boards and the pictures were pasted onto these and labeled to show the water cycle. The idea was that the class would visit the other first-grade class and teach them what they had learned. I sometimes forget that something as small as labeling is a valid writing assignment, and communicating orally with others a powerful extension of learning.

The students now seemed a little more interested in the technical aspects of rain. We never pushed this part of the project, but we increasingly found them brainstorming how and why a particular kind of weather develops. Focusing on how weather affected them as individuals seemed to be helping the children move outward to less personal information.

At the time it seemed that we were doing a lot of direct teaching, but in retrospect I realize we weren't so much conveying information as leading discussions, sharing books and exploring concepts. As teachers, Nora and I were in charge, but we had replaced a transmission model of teaching with one that was transactional. We kept hoping, however, that the children would soon work even more independently.

Severe weather

On my next visit, we discussed severe weather, an important topic in this part of the Midwest, since Springfield and Conway are both in "Tornado Alley." The class had already been thinking about strange weather because, the day before, Nora had read them Judi Barrett's *Cloudy With a Chance of Meatballs,* a story about a town where it rains and snows food. We began by watching an episode of *Reading Rainbow,* the wonderful PBS program that showcases a picture book in each episode and then takes viewers to related topics, as well as reviewing other books on the same topic.

In this episode the host, Levar Burton, focused on severe weather with a visit to the national center for predicting and recording thunderstorms, a reading of *Bringing the Rain to Kapiti Plain,* some wonderful images of lightning and thunder, a mock weather report and a general discussion of rainy-day activities. The previous lesson helped the children understand what was going on and they thoroughly enjoyed the program, itself an exercise in theme exploration.

Afterwards, I asked the students if they had ever been in a storm. They were instantly excited, animated, talkative; every student wanted to talk about his or her experiences. I showed pictures from a full-color book of photographs, *Storms* by Semour Simon, and we talked about what storms might look like — that book has vivid pictures of lightning, tornadoes and hurricanes. Next, we shared a very practical book, Franklyn Branley's *Tornado Alert,* which explains the development of storms, step by step, and tells how people can make sure they are safe. The book is somewhat complicated, but it did help make the point that we shouldn't fear severe weather.

Next, we discussed what we had learned about tornadoes. I shared yet another book, Peter and Connie Roop's *Keep the Lights Burning, Abbie,* which is a true account of a girl who kept a lighthouse going through a terrible storm when her father, the lighthouse keeper, was absent.

It's an "I Can Read Book" that I knew some of the students in the class could handle on their own. (Secretly I was pleased to finally get a little history into our project.)

The children then wrote about their experiences during storms. Many wrote about a tornado which had swept through their county a year or so before and took out the electricity for several days:

> It would problee sand
> Like a volckanoe then I
> Would go down in my
> basement then I didn't
> get hrnt the end
>
> Joshua

> Dear Mr. Chaston
> I lived in Iowa and I saw
> a tornado and my brother
> Adam sead thars a
> Iowa tornado.
>
> Love Melissa

> one day their was a
> terubl stom at my
> houes I was scerd
> me and mom
> went to the basement
> the end.
>
> Danielle

> When I was little there was a Bad
> storm and I was out in my
> clubhouse while the storm was still
> on and I coud not go in the house
> the End
>
> Bradley

Since the class had become so excited during this lesson, I took a more low-key approach the next time I visited. We discussed something that frightens many children: thunder. We had fun talking about some of the silly explanations people have for thunder and lightning. *Tyler Toad and the Thunder,* by Robert Crowe, addresses this fear humorously. The animal friends of T. Tyler Toad, who jumps into a hole whenever it thunders, all have different explanations for what causes the thunder: "the Milky Way Patrol testing their cannons," "the sky animals banging pots and pans," "the big bass drums in the parade across the clouds." But when the thunder returns they, too, jump into the hole.

The children brainstormed their own explanations for thunder, after which I shared another of Franklyn Branley's books, *Flash, Crash, Rumble, and Roll,* which provides insight into the whys of thunder, along with sound ideas about how to be safe in storms.

These two sessions on severe weather were, in many ways, the most exciting of the project, because of the students' genuine interest in and concern about severe weather, something which could only be the result of their own experiences with it. During these lessons, the students also seemed more in control, if only because of their enthusiasm. Their questions directed our topic and they had more choice in their activities.

Variations on a theme

The following week Vickie led the children through a wonderful session on clouds. She began by reminding them of their earlier discussion with Nora about the water cycle, then asked for volunteers to explain the poster they had created. She talked about how water evaporates and goes into the air, condensing into clouds. As in many of our discussions, however, she quickly turned to what mattered to the class, their own feelings about clouds.

She asked the children if they had ever seen pictures in the clouds. They all had: dinosaurs, Big Foot, a car, a Nintendo game, a house and popcorn, among other things. They also described the kinds of clouds they had seen: straight, pink, bumpy, gray, purple, storm clouds, snow clouds. This gave Vickie a chance to introduce Tomie de Paola's *The Cloud Book,* which helps readers identify different kinds of clouds. De Paola's book is funny, informative and within the grasp of young children. It contains folklore (Labrador people once believed that fog was caused by a great white bear who drank so much water that he burst), weather sayings (*Evening red and morning gray/Set the traveler on his way*) and information about what clouds really are ("little drops of water or ice hanging in the upper atmosphere").

After reading that book, Vickie did some good direct teaching using flannel-board cutouts of different kinds of clouds, based on de Paola's illustrations. The students came away with a clear grasp of three different kinds of clouds: cirrus, cumulus and stratus. (She glossed over some of the more exotic kinds such as nimbostratus and cumulonimbus, which the grownups couldn't even keep straight.) Like Nora, Vickie is an excellent, confident teacher.

She concluded by having the students make pictures of clouds out of cottonballs glued to paper. Then they wrote about what their clouds looked like — which ran the gamut from Teenage Mutant Ninja Turtles to one child's grandfather. The children had a lot of fun and Vickie left the flannel-board and cutouts in the classroom so they could play with the cloud figures on other occasions, as they did throughout the rest of the school year.

The next Thursday we had a speaker. The plan had been to bring in a local television weather forecaster, but Vickie knew that the former superintendent of schools had been a weather forecaster in the military, and we invited him instead. The children enjoyed his visit (he had brought slides of Africa to show the kindergarten group the previous year, so they already knew him), but his presentation was somewhat disjointed and way above their heads. I think he realized this, and he later apologized to Vickie. He did, however, help the children see that weather forecasting is real.

During my next visit Nora taught a lesson on rainbows. The day before, the class had made a large rainbow out of poster board, and had been asked to think about what makes rainbows. Pretending that she didn't know herself how a rainbow is made, Nora read some mythological explanations (like the Bifrost Bridge in Norse mythology) and then asked the children to come up with some explanations of their own. One of them suggested that a dragon had sprayed out different-colored flames, another that someone had thrown a series of paint pots up into the sky. As the class shared their ideas, Nora drew pictures on the board to represent them.

She followed this with a discussion of how rainbows are really made, and a science experiment to demonstrate it, using an overhead projector, a dish of water, a flashlight and a mirror. She had trouble getting the rainbow to appear since she hadn't practiced ahead of time, but the class liked it. Then Vickie taught the children the song "You Can Sing a Rainbow," with a taped piano accompaniment by her daughter. Finally, they drew pictures of rainbows and wrote down some of their explanations, both fanciful and realistic:

I think peple afer it rains
some men go up in the sky
in an air plan a take red yellow
and uther colers and theo them down
and make a rainbow. the end
our the rel way is aftier
it rains the sun and the rain hits
to gether and makes a deffunt colors
a made a rainbow

Brandi

Rainbows are
cloufer when I was
little I thought that
the jint was thersty
he was making a
mes he was
dropping koolade

Bradley

I think jueusus makes the rainbow
and you can make a rainbow too.
if you poor a glass of watr and
put it on the ege of the wenbo
and open your hands and then you
have a rainbow the end

Jennifer

My Mom and Dad were
geting redi to paint and
they had red orange
yellow Blue and purple
But then something wird
hapnd they spilt it. And
it went up in to the sky.
And made Rainbow.

Jami

The next Tuesday, March 1, was our "wind" day — brilliant planning, I thought, since we could focus on the old saying: "If March comes in like a lion, it goes out like a lamb," and since the class had made March lions with their art teacher the preceding week and were already disposed to talk about wind.

Once again I introduced the topic through books. We had learned early on that reading aloud to the children not only got them reading the same books on their own, but also provided them all with the same background information, regardless of reading ability.

The books we used this time included Arnold Lobel's *Frog and Toad All Year,* which has a story about kites, and Patricia McKissack's *Mirandy and Brother Wind,* a Caldecott Honor book containing a literary folktale drawn from Afro-American culture. I didn't read the latter aloud but merely showed the pictures and summarized the story, in which Mirandy sets out to capture Brother Wind so he can be her partner in the junior cakewalk, and asked the children if they thought anyone could really capture the wind in a barn as Mirandy does. Then we read some poems about wind, including "Who Has Seen the Wind?" Afterwards, we talked about what causes wind and why we can't see it.

The students produced some excellent writing in response to our discussion. Since they had enjoyed writing poems about rain, we decided to give poetry another try, this time using each of the five senses to describe wind. (I admit to being heavily influenced by Kenneth Koch's *Rose, Where Did You Get That Red?*) To help them develop a word bank, we brainstormed words that describe how the wind sounds, feels, looks, smells and even tastes. Then we wrote poems, a line at a time, with individual students borrowing words and ideas if they needed them. This process gave them the direction and help they needed but allowed them to be creative — and to incorporate both science and literature. The children were excited about sharing their poems, and in my mind this was one of the best moments of the project.

the wind
like this ooooh
ooooh
it would be white
it would be could
it would smaill
like smoek

Heather

I think the wind sound like this
oooooooooooooooh I see wind going By
I think it tastlike coldnes
I think it tast like berte
I sied I don't think my sister tasted
the wind defor and me nether the end

Jennifer

The windy day
shooooo! goes the wind.
when its a windy day the trees boue.
It fells sorta fluffy coldish.
I smel flowers.
The wind is sweet to taste.

Brandi

A wind wind day
Wind Wind go
a way come
back a nothr
day
woooh

Brandon

The wind sound like win you are
in a car. I mite see a bas boll hat
fly off. It fils very woorm. It smels
like folorws. It tasts like minr.

Jami

The Maggick Wind.
Wish we cann't see the
wind. it is could and soft.
it smales like carits.
it taset like baby food
and Sarah tasted
she sed it taset gros.

Melissa

The Wind's
The wind suous like this: ouow.
I would see a cap blow.
I thaink it's cod and hot.
Is smls like fars.

Amber

Hooow. the wind wild look
lice little lines.
the wind fils cowld.
sometimes I smel a scuinge.

Jeff

After missing a week for spring break, at our next
meeting we followed up our discussion of wind by dealing
with air. I had intended to make kites, but the children
seemed more interested in paper airplanes. As a result, after
using another Branley book, *Air Is All Around You,* Vickie
helped the class to create paper airplanes. Hoping to discuss
air currents, she divided the class into groups and had one
member from each group throw his or her airplane. The
others then measured the distance. It was very windy and
difficult to throw straight, but the children really liked the
event and decided to write newspaper articles about it.
After we discussed the kinds of information their readers
would need, each child wrote an account of what
happened. Here are two examples:

Our class went outside and flew paper airplanes and the farthest paper airplane was Jeremy Week's. Our team only got 200 and 70 inches. The other team only got 37 inches. Number three got 400 and 91 inches. There team won. We lost. We had fun and even Mr. Chaston flew a paper airplane.

Jami

Miss Wolf's class went outside and flew airplanes. Nathan's airplane hit me in the head when he started to fly it. Jeremy flew his airplane and then we went inside and Jeremy's airplane flew 491 miles and won.

Rachelle

For the remainder of the project time we tied up loose ends. We talked further about weather forecasting, listed other old sayings they knew about weather, and read *I Can Be a Weather Forecaster* by Claire Martin. We looked back at the materials we had used throughout the project and reviewed what we had learned. The students talked about their favorite books and activities. They wrote me letters telling me about some of the things they remembered or had enjoyed. Some wrote more stories, real and imaginary, about weather.

During this time we also had a chance to look back over the children's writing. Under most circumstances, they would have edited their work along the way, but given my limited schedule, it had been next to impossible to find time to edit and rewrite on a regular basis. We had discovered that for first-graders editing requires a great deal of direction, and I spent time working with some of the students one on one. In many cases that meant little more than figuring out the inventive spellings. Unfortunately, some of the students didn't remember what it was they had written.

But I was pleased with many of things they had done, particularly their rain and wind poems. They had also written some interesting stories about severe weather. A few students hadn't completed more than a few words, but

I felt that the writing activities in general had been successful, particularly since the class had a high number of children with learning disabilities and one student who spoke little English.

My last "official" visit to Nora's class was on Thursday, April 10, when I took them the finished copies of the classroom book they had created — the same day they were taking a national standardized reading test! A day of irony in which, sandwiched between tests, I was presenting the culmination of our efforts to avoid rigid, programmed teaching. Ironic, but perhaps typical.

When I showed them the book, the children immediately began counting to compare how many times their work appeared. Although all of them were represented, it hadn't been possible to represent them all equally. Some had simply not produced enough. But even the ESL student who had come from India and spoke little English made some contribution: hers was the cover illustration.

Before the Rainbow:
Weather Poems and Stories

by Mrs. Nora Wolf's
First Grade Class
1989–90
Ezard Elementary School

Edited by Dr. Joel Chaston

Great ideas abandoned

As with the fourth-grade project, many of our most "spectacular" ideas were eventually abandoned, sometimes because of time, sometimes because of the nature of the first-grade students, and sometimes because their interests led us in different directions.

Ongoing student editing

As I mentioned, I had originally planned to have the students edit their writing throughout the project. I knew instinctively that editing was an important part of the writing process, but even though the students enjoyed writing and had been writing all year, they weren't especially interested in anything beyond a first draft. Furthermore, my time in the classroom was too limited. In the end, other than occasional revisions of specific aspects of their work, we settled for helping them learn to ask questions about what they had written and to rethink their work after reading it aloud. Nora was especially good at asking questions about their writing.

Weather experiments and the science fair

When we began the project, we intended to stress the scientific and technological aspects of whatever subject we finally chose. I had some wonderful material on weather — I was especially eager to try some of the experiments in Valerie Wyatt's *Weather Watch*. Some of the experiments, however, were fairly sophisticated for first-graders. With another group and more time we might indeed have collected a tornado, made a thunderstorm, or acted as human thermometers. The children might also have done something in connection with the school's science fair.

We had also considered encouraging the students to keep weather logs, charting and mapping weather changes. They seemed moderately interested in this, but we never quite found the time to do it. And in the end they guided us away from the scientific aspects of the subject.

Class newspaper

Early on, we discussed developing a class newspaper in which the children would record weather experiments and present factual material about weather. As the project seemed to grow more and more towards creative and personal writing, however, the class booklet supplanted that idea.

Creative drama and music

The children clearly enjoyed the choral reading we did, as well as the song Vickie taught them. They would probably have liked acting out some of the stories we read. *The Snowy Day, Tyler Toad and the Thunder* and *Cloudy With a Chance of Meatballs* all seem good candidates for creative drama. There is also an abundance of weather-related music, everything from "Night on Bald Mountain" to "Singing in the Rain" and "Itsy Bitsy Spider." Perhaps if we had spent more time brainstorming the kinds of activities the children would like to pursue in connection with weather, they might have asked for some of these activities.

Group projects

I had always wanted the students to work more in groups. They did read books to each other and sometimes share their writing, but in general large-group discussions took over, once again partly because of time and logistics. Because some students were pulled out for special classes, the large group was at times rather small. Throughout the project, however, the children continued to share opinions about some of the weather-related books they were reading.

Summary

All in all, I was pleased with what happened at Conway. Although we had our share of failures, we were successful in getting the children excited about writing and reading in a specific content area.

However, the project drove home to me the difficulties of public school teaching: tight schedules, outside distractions, different levels of ability among the students. I also realized that whole language teaching has to be more than a single unit grafted onto the curriculum of a class. It would have helped if I had been in the classroom more often, so that I could build on what the children learned during the rest of the day. Our project was, perhaps, only a step above a thematic unit, though moving towards the idea of theme cycles.

For a while I was worried that we hadn't "empowered" our students with the opportunity to make decisions about what they learned, but I'm now convinced that there was a great deal of choice along the way. The children chose many of the topics we discussed, what books they would read on their own, and which stories and poems we would include in the classroom book.

I also wondered if we inundated them with too much factual material and too many books. Did we make them feel like the characters in *Cloudy With a Chance of Meatballs*? Those sorry people were almost buried by a storm of meatballs, pancakes and fried eggs, and finally had to flee to another country. Were the children being smothered by poetry and science — metaphors and meteorology?

But while we were not always successful in what we did, the children clearly enjoyed the unit and most of the reading and writing they did. In the end I realized that we had indeed successfully practiced many of the principles of whole language teaching. In many ways Nora's classroom was already a whole language classroom. Despite the fact that her curriculum was, of necessity, sometimes very traditional, her treatment of her students, her efforts to encourage their creativity, her respect for their ideas fit everything I feel about whole language.

I view what we did as a form of what Donald Murray and Lucy Calkins call "rehearsal." In *The Art of Teaching Writing,* Calkins says that "Rehearsal is, above all, a way of living." (p.17) Her rehearsal for the book she was writing had taken place twelve years before. We, too, were rehearsing and growing, trying to become whole language teachers, discovering that in many ways we already were.

Our students were not forced to be robots — or to write about them either. Instead, in our journey through metaphors and meteorology, we learned that the basic principles of whole language *do* work in an ordinary classroom, though not without a lot of work.

Whole language principles in action: Fourth-grade retrospect

In chapter three we referred to various whole language principles as goals towards which whole language teachers strive. In this chapter and the next, we will select some of the principles most clearly actualized in our theme exploration projects and demonstrate how they were actualized. We will use the same headings we used earlier, but it's important to remember that many of the topics naturally fit in more than one category. For example, examples of teachers and students negotiating the curriculum logically belong under the categories dealing with all three: learners, teachers and curriculum. Furthermore, since joint decision-making requires the assessment of needs, interests and possibilities, assessment is involved as well.

Scott ~ Learning and the learner

Earlier we described how education can be either transmitted to or transacted by the learner. Before embarking on this project I was firmly camped in the transmission model, but without quite realizing it. I was an energetic, committed and often highly motivating teacher, but one who was nevertheless always in control. Following the curriculum, I handed information, knowledge and concepts to my students. I could deliver the information pretty well. I could make the subject matter interesting and I was good at conjuring up images and ideas in my students' minds out of the material I gave them. But I was still force-feeding them knowledge that they might or might not have an intrinsic desire to learn.

As we began our theme exploration, my prime goal was to jettison the transmission model of learning from my classroom. No longer did I want to fill my students' heads with knowledge that *I* wanted them to learn. No longer did I want to see the knowledge I had worked so hard to transfer to my students drip through as fast as I could put it in, like water through a sieve. I wanted them not merely to digest knowledge I handed to them on a textbook platter, but also to determine the menu and prepare the food, then consume their own self-selected, self-prepared meal. I wanted them to seek answers to questions they viewed as important and relevant to their lives; the process of seeking answers would have as much effect as the answers themselves, I felt. I believed that one question would lead to others and would stretch to form a continuous pattern of self-generated learning.

Perhaps Alice Walker in her fine novel *The Color Purple* best sums up the quality I was looking for when she points out that in wondering about the big things, people learn a lot about the little things as well. This kind of learning model leads to a different type of learning — a deeper, stronger learning that withstands the witherings of time and alters the way learners view the world long after they leave the classroom.

The following passages from Gary Paulsen's novel *The Island* clarify the kind of teaching I wanted to abandon, and the kind of learning I wanted to facilitate in my classroom. Having discovered an uninhabited island, 14-year-old Wil Newton spends day after day there, observing nature in minute detail and writing about his observations. One of his pieces deals with a frog. Wil begins:

Once in biology, before we did fetal pigs, we had to dissect frogs. We cut their little bellies open and all looked at their little intestines and little stomachs and little hearts and little eyes and little brains and when we did this we were supposed to learn two things — we were supposed to learn and know all about frogs, and we were supposed to learn and be amazed at the "miracle of life." . . .

But later, on the island, I saw a heron suddenly snake its head down and grab a frog — not spear but grab; they don't spear with their beaks — and flip it around in the air twice to get it positioned right and swallow it down, alive, straightening its throat to take the still live, still kicking frog down into its stomach. And I thought then that from biology I learned almost absolutely nothing about frogs except how their guts looked and that is next to nothing. (p. 119)

So Wil decided to spend a day observing a frog, describing what it looked like, what it did, how it reacted in fear when a water snake swam past apparently looking for dinner, and how it sang to attract a mate but instead attracted another male frog, who scrambled for possession of the log. Wil concludes his dissertation on the frog:

Then he sang again and this time the song was a small bit different, perhaps a bit lower and louder. He had felt anger and had fought and had felt fear of the snake and had defended his territory and I thought two things, two things from the time with the frog. I thought: Where does that show, where does the fear and anger and pride and song show when you are poking in the frog's gut with a stick and where, I thought, is the frog different from me? (p. 122)

Note the difference between the stale, lifeless knowledge acquired in the classroom and the power and intensity of the knowledge acquired on the learner's own terms. I wanted to encourage the latter kind of learning among my students and in my classroom by giving them more control over their learning. Beyond the initiating activities, I set out with no activities or outcomes in mind. The students were free to choose the paths they wanted to pursue within the framework of the theme, and putting them in the driver's seat created more sparks, more interest and more curiosity than would normally have been the case. The following entry from my journal, written after the class divided into their groups for the first time, captures some of the excitement generated by this student-centered learning.

March 15

Today we broke into groups for the first time, and the kids began to make in earnest the plans they hoped to follow, to examine all the possibilities that lay before them. Up to this point, everything was merely setting the groundwork, getting the machine ready to move. But today the wheels actually began to turn and the machine to gain its own momentum. It can't be stopped now.

In a way, I find this very comforting. The real project had not begun until now. All we had done were readiness activities, and at the back of my mind there was always the possibility that things would sputter and shut down before anything really got started. After today's meeting, however, that possibility went out the window, for today I saw the light in the children's eyes.

Let me define that light, for it is not a new experience to me. This light is an extremely bright, clarifying light that shines in my own mind when I come across an idea that I know will work in my classroom. It's a light that comes from my enthusiasm and excitement, creating interest in my students. It radiates from me like heat from a wood stove, catches students in its warm glow, and carries things along to a successful conclusion.

There was something very different about today, however. The light I saw and felt was shining from *their* eyes and wrapping me in its glow. This time my students were carrying me along. I was the one being sucked in by *their* enthusiasm.

This came about while I was working with the environment group. The kids were brainstorming different ideas and topics they could study. Acid rain, oil spills, ozone depletion rolled off their tongues. They tossed out ideas about different projects they could develop to display their new-found knowledge. Slowly it dawned on them that they were in charge, they were the key decision-makers. I would merely provide them with the materials and resources they would need. As this novel concept began to sink in, the glow began to radiate from their eyes and warm me. I could feel the engine kick into life, with the learners behind the wheel. I know there is no turning back.

Nature and development of the curriculum

It should be fairly obvious that the curriculum that was negotiated in both classrooms was expressive of the kinds of learning experiences that engage lifelong learners outside of school: discussing topics of interest, reading novels and doing experiments, for example. And of course that curriculum focused on an exploration of topics or themes. What we want to illustrate in more detail is how we supported the students' learning by providing a wide range of resources, how we negotiated curriculum, and how we taught or developed skills in context. In each case we hope our specific examples will illuminate whole language principles.

Literature and other reading materials

One of the biggest challenges in exploring a theme is providing resources for the students so they can pursue independent research. Libraries can't entirely fill the need. Even though we live in a community blessed with two well-stocked public library systems and a major university, if we had relied solely on these traditional sources, our project would quickly have ground to a halt. Nor would we have tapped into the wealth of information and expertise available in other areas of the community.

Finding resources for a thematic unit is much like fishing: you drop in a line and reel in everything you catch. You don't limit yourself to one place, either, but keep moving around until every resource in the community has been plumbed to its depth. Our sources, for example, ranged from library books to the local phone directory, from posters to the educational junk mail that crossed our desks, from a new local environmental magazine to a placemat from a nationally known fast-food chain.

Fishing throughout the community also provided us with resources from some decidedly non-traditional sources. Here is a partial list of our "catch":

~ Bestsellers
The Earth Day 1990 celebration took books off the science shelf and onto the bestseller list. Two from the Earth Works Group were eminently helpful in the environment project: *50 Simple Things You Can Do to Save the Earth* and *50 Simple Things Kids Can Do to Save the Earth*. Another, *Future Stuff* (Abrams and Bernstein), was especially valuable for the technology group.

~ Magazines
The Michigan United Conservation Clubs publish *Tracks*, a nature magazine for children. The Earth Day 1990 edition of this magazine provided a child's-eye view of the complex problems that face the environment. We also found a newly created local magazine called *With the Grain*, two sections of which proved especially helpful: "Young Minds," a collection of children's activities centering around specific issues such as acid rain; and "First Steps," a section at the end of each article containing simple, concrete activities that amplify the ideas discussed in the article.

~ Earth Day 1990
On April 22, 1990, various environmental groups from the area gathered in a downtown Kalamazoo park to celebrate Earth Day. The pamphlets and suggestions gathered at this celebration were very helpful to the environment project.

~ Posters
Two posters served as invaluable resources for the environment group. The first was actually one large poster subdivided into smaller pictures of endangered

species. On the back we found background information about the animals and the causes for their near extinction, which the students used as a basis for a series of reports on endangered species. The second was a free poster promoting Earth Day 1990, included in a packet of fliers advertising new science curriculum materials. The back was filled with a series of experiments centered around Earth Day themes, and these proved to be excellent additions to the environment group's projects.

~ Speakers
The social concerns group organized presentations to the whole class on several topics: a temporary shelter for teens, drinking and driving (given by a young man who had been permanently crippled by a drunk driver), and the disease of alcoholism. The young man, soon afterwards elected president of MADD (Mothers Against Drunk Driving), also brought brochures.

~ Annotated bibliographies
The independent nature of the projects meant that the students were constantly seeking new sources of information. Annotated bibliographies allowed them to be more selective and efficient in their search. The titles of some of those bibliographies are listed on pages 193-195. One the students found very helpful was Jim Trelease's *The Read-Aloud Handbook*.

Connie ~ Negotiating the curriculum

The phrase "negotiating the curriculum" is perhaps unfortunate, since it calls forth images of collective bargaining: students presenting their demands, teachers countering with theirs, and the two groups posturing as adversaries until some compromises are reached, perhaps accompanied by an aftermath of bitterness. But nothing could be further from the spirit of a whole language classroom.

In actual practice, negotiating the curriculum means that teachers and students brainstorm possibilities and make curricular decisions together in an atmosphere of collaboration and accommodation. In addition, the teacher remains alert and sensitive to the developing interests and needs of the students, and initial intentions and plans may give way to take advantage of these new interests and meet the new needs. When teachers deliberately enlist the students as joint decision-makers and develop an attitude and atmosphere of responsiveness, the issue of control rarely arises.

We already indicated in chapter three some of the ways we negotiated the curriculum: providing introductory activities, brainstorming concerns they might want to address, grouping and categorizing their responses, guiding them in choosing a group and a topic to work with, and working with each group to reach agreement about their final project. Typically, these instances involved an ebb and flow between teacher and students, with the teacher suggesting initial possibilities, the students offering other possibilities and concrete examples, the teacher responding to the students' ideas, the students making individual and group decisions and, finally, the teacher indicating agreement and approval.

We also described examples of how, in a sense, the curriculum was renegotiated on an ongoing basis in response to the students' interests and needs as they arose — for example, when I accommodated my group's eagerness to start thinking about props for their play and to start acting out scenes when they'd done little more than outline them. The following journal entries and reflections provide further examples.

March 27

Today in trying to make decisions regarding the characters of our play we debated whether drug dealers would be dressed shabbily or well. Amanda and Brandy argued for "scruffy," while I suggested that drug dealers might be better dressed, since they make a lot of money from drug sales. The result of the discussion was that Amanda, Brandy and Jenny wanted to do a survey to see what the class thought, expecting that we would then act upon the majority's belief in creating the characters in our play. I pointed out that we were supposed to be gaining information and sharing it, that our final decision should be based upon solid knowledge rather than upon opinion that might or might not be well founded. The girls wanted to go to the other fourth-grade classes and take a survey. I reluctantly said that was fine if Mr. Peterson okayed it. He did, so they took the survey before Thursday's class.

With splendid hindsight, I now wish I had been more enthusiastic about their idea. In effect, I could have treated the survey as a *prediction* that we might find confirmed or not when we delved more deeply.

Obviously the idea of renegotiating the curriculum daily takes some getting used to, and a willingness to reconsider and tolerate students' ideas for activities that initially seem of dubious value. I am gradually coming to accept the fact that we teachers don't always know what will constitute valuable learning experiences for our students. We must let them make more of their own choices in order to maximize their learning.

April 10

I distributed a copy of the outline of our play, a copy on which I had written the names of which kids I'd like to have write each scene. My intention was to be sure that the team for each scene included someone who would be acting in the scene, as well as someone who was supposed to be an "expert" on the topic(s) reflected in that scene: child abuse, alcoholism, running away from home, whatever. Before making out this list, I debated how to deal with the fact that two kids who were good friends tended to dominate discussion and try to get their own way in decisions made by the group. Finally I decided to put these two girls together for writing two scenes, and to separate them for writing two others.

I explained my rationale to the kids, but sure enough, the most domineering of the students complained about not working with her friend. I pointed out that they were scheduled to work together on two of the four scenes they'd be involved with, and dismissed the group.

April 12

Despite my original assertiveness in assigning students to write particular scenes, I was somewhat uncomfortable with my unilateral decision-making. After all, we were supposed to be negotiating the curriculum together!

Thus, today, I think I may have been the one who reopened the question of who should write what scenes, by asking if they were satisfied with what I'd suggested or whether they would prefer to keep the same team of three people, with each team writing three or four scenes of the eleven we had outlined. Finally we took a vote, which turned out 4 to 4. To break the tie, the kids wanted to call Jeni, who was home ill, but Scott said no. We discussed the alternatives and voted again, this time with eyes shut. The vote was still 4 to 4. So the kids suggested that I break the tie. I decided we should reorganize in consistent teams of three.

The kids then regrouped themselves, once again attending to who would be acting in what scene — and I reminded them to try to include an "expert," though by now everyone was becoming somewhat knowledgeable about everything anyhow. Of course the two girls who tended to dominate chose to work in the same group of three.

This is another example, I think, of my initially having difficulty letting go of teacher control, partly because I had in mind certain requirements for each team of writers, and partly because I thought sheer chaos might result if the students were to decide who would work with whom. Also, I had some lingering sense of "teacher knows best." When I relinquished control and let the students choose their own writing groups, the project actually began to proceed more smoothly.

One might wonder why I was willing to spend so much valuable group time making a simple decision, but this democratic process is not only an important part of the product — that is, what children learn from their schooling — but also an important characteristic of whole language classrooms.

May 30

[Tim Smith, a director of children's theater, is the person I had talked into rehearsing the play with the kids. Since he wasn't able to be with us the last week of rehearsals, I took over the directing.]

One of the interesting differences between Tim and me is that Tim hasn't been willing to listen to the kids' suggestions for improving the play, while I am. Here is an example of how we "negotiated" today.

In the final scene, after the mother and father admit that they need some counseling help, Tim suggested that the family join hands in a happy circle. I thought that looked hokey, since a real family wouldn't do that. So I suggested that the dad put his arm around the mother and the mother put her arm around the girls — a sort of semi-circle. Brian fussed about doing that, though, because he thought it looked funny with him putting his arm around Jeni, who is so much taller.

At the time, I more or less insisted that my change was an improvement. However, I kept thinking about the problem and concluded that one way to respond to Brian's concern while still avoiding the handholding would be to have Jeni sit down and Brian come over and put his hand on her shoulder. Just as in the earlier scenes, then, the father would *appear* taller than the mother.

To me, this incident seems to exemplify what's meant by "negotiating the curriculum." Yes, I made the final decision (until the producer later improved upon it!), but I took the student's concern seriously and made modifications accordingly.

Again, when confronted with a student's suggestion — or in this case, objection — my quick reaction was to insist upon doing things my own way. But at least I am learning to listen to the students, consider their ideas, and, usually, find some way to accommodate their interests or concerns. This is often what happens in my college classes, too. In recent years I have found it easier and easier to allow, even to encourage, more of a student role in decision-making.

Connie ~ Skills in context

Whole language teachers teach skills in context. Teachers who haven't internalized the whole language philosophy may interpret "context" in a narrow way: teaching vocabulary within the context of a sentence or a paragraph, for instance. However, more experienced whole language teachers interpret this principle more broadly. They discuss appropriate strategies when the students are having difficulties reading, explain a needed convention of writing while the students are editing their work, and so forth. Various literacy and life skills are taught *within the context of an authentic literacy event or learning experience,* and in response to the students' needs and the demands of the tasks they are undertaking.

We described earlier how Scott guided his students in learning to use the table of contents to locate book annotations in the bibliography *Adventuring with Books* (Jett-Simpson). The following journal entries provide further examples of teaching skills in context, including an anecdote that suggests it isn't always the best thing to do!

March 1

I was impressed with the way Scott integrated the development of writing skills into the activity of choosing a group (topic). He had prepared a sheet on which the kids were to give their first choice of groups and explain why, then do the same for their second choice and indicate if there was any topic they really did *not* want.

He said we needed to have the groups roughly equal, so the students wouldn't necessarily get their first choice. Therefore, it was important to be as detailed as they could about why they wanted the group they specified as their first choice. He gave some examples, too, of the kinds of reasons they might offer. Great tactic for encouraging detail in their persuasive writing!

The following examples illustrate not only the teaching of skills in context, but also the negotiating of curriculum. The writing is functional and purposeful for the learner.

Survey

Name Jerome H
3-1-90

① Of the three groups we have discussed, what is your first choice? Technology! . Why would you like to belong to this group? What would you like to study and why? etc.

I like this group because I like Electronics. It is nice to study. I like building thing with wires and other thing and, so do my brothers & sisters. We always try to make jetpacks superfasebike's and alls thing. I would would like being in the Technology group because I like it I would like to study computers, cats, & Hous

② If you can't be a member of your "first-choice" group, what would be your second choice? Who Socal

what would you like to study in this group and why I would like to be in the social group because it's helping the people & their problems. I would like to help the people that are on drugs. Of course in in my sels but with other people who want a help.

③ Is there a group you would not like to belong to? Why? _____

Any of the groups are
fine
for
ME!

Survey

Name Matthew

① Of the three groups we have discussed, what is your first choice? Technology . Why would you like to belong to this group? What would you like to study and why? etc.

I would like Cars, computers, or houses. I like cars because I im wonjest what cars of the future would be like. I like comput because my mother knows a lot about comp ter, I'm interested. I'm houses because my father is a bulder. He knows a lot about hous of the future.

② If you can't be a member of your "first-choice" group, what would be your second choice? Enviorment

what would you like to study in this group and why? I I did a research of the environment. I'd like to do it on polution. I'd do polution because its very interesting. I could earn a lot about the futre in polition

③ Is there a group you would not like to belong to? Why? Social

I dont want social because it would be boring to to me now.

Survey

Name Bahra

① Of the three groups we have discussed, what is your first choice? social . Why would y like to belong to this group? What would you like to study and why? etc.

I would like to be in the social group bec I watch tv. a lot and I see thing on the tv about child abuse suiside ect. Drugs is what consecns me the most. One tv. it showed a baby that her mother was a druggie it was shaking and it looked sick I stured to cry. I feel very strong about Drugs

② If you can't be a member of your "first-choice" group, what would be your second choice? Who Environment

what would you like to study in this group and why? I would also like to be in the environment but not as much. Oil spills consern me the most in the enviroment. I was wacting tv. again the Donahue show \ Ted Dansine was on it and he was talking about the oil spill He said "It's easy all they have to do is covers

③ Is there a group you would not like to belong to? Why? technology

I don't want to be in the technology group. Ever since I was 4 I was afraid of all those little graphics ect. I stared to scream.

~ 130 ~

March 22

I wanted to work on research skills with three students: Maria, who had already done some reading in her novel on child abuse; Jeni, who couldn't decide whether she wanted to deal with suicide or the homeless; and Jill, who had chosen child abuse but did not yet have a book to read. I had brought seven Kalamazoo telephone books (different years, different versions) and I asked the kids where we'd look to find people who might help us learn about their topics. Could we look in the white pages? They quickly realized that we couldn't, unless we knew exactly what agency or person we wanted to call. Then where should we look in the yellow pages?

We first tried a specific topic, in this case child abuse. One book had a cross-reference under that heading, but the others had nothing. So I suggested that we needed a broader topic. What might work? Maria suggested social groups, which was close enough to "social organizations" to work. I had also photocopied several pages of community service listings from a phone book of a couple years ago. We looked at that together, deciding which categories and which agencies under those categories looked promising. Drawing upon my prior knowledge as well as our inferences from the listings, we together chose agencies to call for information and/or speakers on child abuse and runaways, alcohol and drug abuse, and suicide prevention.

Because this mini-lesson was conducted within the context of the students' current need for information on their topics, it was much more useful than an isolated lesson on using the yellow pages. Furthermore, teaching this skill in the context of their research project should enhance the retention of salient details — for example, how to find alternative or broader topic headings when you can't find something specific listed.

April 24

While my students were writing their play, composing in groups on the computers in the computer lab, an interesting incident happened that illustrates the importance of not trying to teach certain kinds of skills while students are in the throes of drafting. Occasionally, while composing, Brian would ask me how to spell a difficult word and I'd oblige, seeing no good reason to insist that he use invented spelling for this first draft when someone was handy to help. Well, one day he asked the laboratory assistant how to spell a word. She immediately got a dictionary and told him to look it up. While he was looking, Mary explained to me that she really believes in using a dictionary and always encourages the kids to use one whenever they want to know how to spell something. I quietly indicated that I encourage students just to spell the best they can — or in some cases give them the spelling — when they're composing, so the flow of writing isn't disrupted. Time enough later for revising and editing.

As so often happens, Brian tried to find the word (whatever it was) but couldn't, so he just handed the dictionary back to Mary and wrote a simpler word instead. Lesson learned. The next week Mary began giving the kids the spelling rather than handing them the dictionary while they were in the heat of composition.

Connie ~ Teacher roles in facilitating learning

Two of the most significant ways whole language teachers facilitate learning we already discussed under the heading of curriculum:

~ They teach skills not in isolation, but within the context of authentic literacy and learning experiences.

~ They negotiate and renegotiate the curriculum with students in response to their interests and needs.

But teachers have other critical functions as well:

~ They are organizers extraordinaire, allotting time to activities and projects, helping students group themselves and organize their work, keeping records, locating resources and supplies.

~ They work to create a supportive community of learners, where individual differences are respected and collaboration is promoted.

~ They expect excellence from each student according to his or her ability, and demonstrate that expectation in daily interactions with all students.

In addition to these general characteristics of whole language teachers, we want to illustrate several specific teacher roles that support learning.

Role-modeling

A whole language teacher *demonstrates* by openly sharing what it means to be a reader, a writer and a lifelong learner. This is an awesome responsibility. It means that teachers need to be people who read voluntarily, both for pleasure and out of curiosity to learn more about their world. They need to be eager rather than reluctant writers, sharing their own enthusiasm for coming to know through writing and for expressing and communicating their ideas. They need to be lifelong learners, using their skill with the written and spoken word to enhance and enrich their own lives.

How Scott demonstrates the attributes of a lifelong learner is revealed in the following journal entry.

February 22

Scott is a wonderful model of how to teach effectively, as suggested not only by my comments on his teaching procedures, but also by the sophistication of the students' responses to questions like "How could you make the world a more beautiful place?" They have learned a tremendous amount from him between September and now.

What's interesting is how he accomplishes this teaching: in many ways, indirectly. Supposedly, he teaches them only language arts; but he shares his own reading about environmental and other social concerns with the kids, and they learn through his enthusiastic sharing. He models what it is to be an inquiring, lifelong learner — and they emulate.

Other types of demonstration include the teacher reading while the students are reading, and writing while the students are writing. For example, when the students wrote their responses to "How could you make the world a more beautiful place?" I wrote too; when they wrote descriptions of what they heard, saw, felt and smelled on the playground, both Scott and I wrote our own descriptions, and Scott shared his with the class. And, of course, we both read a great deal of fiction and nonfiction on the topics our groups were exploring. We read and wrote and discussed and shared as part of the community of learners.

The power of teacher demonstration was revealed perhaps most poignantly when some of the students in my group wanted to start carrying their project materials in a briefcase like mine. Clearly, students attach significance to whatever teachers model for them — and also, unfortunately, to what teachers neglect to model.

Facilitating

One way teachers stimulate learning is by suggesting specific learning experiences: topics to research, projects to undertake, books to read, experiments to conduct. They also engage the students in activities and discussions that generate interest and develop a knowledge base — for instance, my reading of *Miss Rumphius* and two chapters of *Norby*. And if I had proceeded with it, the improvisational drama might have encouraged speculation about the problems of society and research into the promise of robot technology.

Sharing knowledge and experience

As the following journal entry shows, the sharing whole language teachers do is far different from the traditional teaching of facts and skills.

May 16

Yesterday I spoke with Melissa, who had only one word to say throughout the entire play before Tim rewrote the last scene to give her a few more lines. I suggested that we needed someone to introduce the play on the videotape and said that might be a good job for her. She agreed to think about what she might say and maybe jot down some ideas.

Today we worked on drafting the introduction. We brainstormed well together, both realizing that, for starters, we needed to tell why we had done this play. I suggested that we also needed to tell who we (they) are. Then I thought of checking out the five W's — who, what, when, where and why — and how. This helped us focus our thinking. Sometimes I was concerned that I was being too pushy about foisting my ideas onto Melissa, and at one point I even asked her. She said "No" and seemed to mean it, so after that I felt comfortable with my suggestions.

I guess I see my "suggestions" in situations like this as a sort of modeling or demonstrating. How are the kids supposed to know everything if someone more experienced doesn't share what he/she knows? Melissa had some good ideas, too, so writing the introduction to the play really was a collaborative effort.

Situations like this clarify one of the crucial differences between direct teaching in traditional classrooms and teaching in whole language classrooms. Whole language teachers teach, and often do so directly, but usually even their direct teaching is subtle because it occurs in the context of need. Sharing information in the context of a collaborative project is just one instance of that kind of subtle teaching. In addition to being more practical than facts and information offered in a vacuum, such information is imparted in an atmosphere of collegiality that enhances its likelihood of being grasped, retained and used on other occasions as appropriate.

Assisting learners in using what they know

Sometimes a related and important function of the teacher is just helping students use what they already know, as the following journal entry indicates.

April 24

At first, when my group began writing the play, I had to give the kids a lot of help: with play format (ways of indicating stage directions as opposed to dialogue, for example), with information to make the play more realistic (for example, I suggested that the alcoholic mother might be more likely to drink vodka than beer), and in general with trying to think like the characters. Again and again I'd ask: "If you were so-and-so, how do you think you'd feel? What do you think you'd say?" Of course, their reading of novels on their chosen topic also helped somewhat with thinking and feeling and speaking like the characters. Interestingly, perhaps the hardest part of my job was to get the kids to use in their play some of the information they'd learned about alcoholism and child abuse. Perhaps these situations are still not real enough to them — thank goodness!

Collaborating

The way I worked with the group to develop the script for the play and with Melissa to develop the introduction for the videotape illustrates how teachers can work collaboratively with their students. It also illustrates how they can serve as a developmental editor for their students.

During group discussion, the group decided on the order of scenes. I typed the outline for everyone, adding a couple of scenes I thought would require the students to draw more on the information they found concerning their respective topics. The students then wrote the play, though not in strict chronological order; each group had three or four scenes to write, determined mainly by what scenes they would be acting in. As the first draft neared completion, I suggested omitting two scenes that now seemed repetitious — including one I had originally suggested. Once all the scenes had been drafted, I edited the entire play. If I'd had more time I would have consulted the students about the few substantive revisions I made, but as it turned out I simply solicited their approval afterwards.

My function, therefore, was both collaborator and developmental editor, but not dictator. This process nicely illustrates the ebb and flow between teacher and students that characterizes how whole language teachers and their students continually renegotiate curriculum.

Guiding discussion and research

On a day-to-day basis, one of the most important ways whole language teachers stimulate learning is by guiding their students in discussing and thinking.

Particularly during the exploration of a topic or theme, teachers can guide their students' thinking by encouraging them to brainstorm questions they want answered. Some teachers do this by inviting and guiding the creation of three lists: a list of "what we already know about the topic" encourages the students to recall relevant prior knowledge and experience; a list of "what we want to know" motivates reading and investigation; a list of "what we learned" summarizes the information they acquire as their research progresses. This is the K-W-L strategy Scott mentioned earlier.

In this case we simply discussed the topics of interest and pooled our knowledge informally. Then we brainstormed the questions we wanted answered. These questions helped prompt our reading and, for the environmental group, the choice of experiments they undertook.

Notes
Kristen don't forget what you said at CCD.
(1) What is air Pollution?
(2) What are some problems?
Eyes sting, buildings / some metal, paint peels
(3) What does it harm? Plants
(4) How is it made?
(5) Is their anyway to stop it
(6) How does it harm your health
(7) what is acid rain?
(8) How to cars pollution?
(9) How can fact. stop?
(10) How can cars stop?

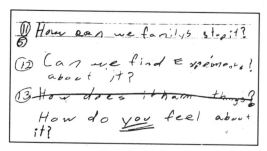

Teachers also stimulate learning by guiding their students step-by-step through new processes. For instance, Scott's students learned precisely how to use a table of contents and how to include sensory detail in their journal entries, while I helped mine learn how to find what they needed in the yellow pages and how to take notes while watching a videotape.

Relating new information to old

Although it logically fits under the preceding heading, drawing upon the students' prior knowledge and helping them relate new information to old is such an important activity that it deserves a heading and generous illustration of its own. Again the best examples come from journal entries.

April 10

We had a guest speaker, Leonard Marcilous, from The Ark. We got off to a good start, I think, by the way I introduced Leonard. I told the kids he was with The Ark, then asked what they remembered about the Ark in the Bible. Of course they remembered it was a ship, and that animals were loaded onto it in pairs. I had to keep prompting to elicit *why* the animals were taken onto the Ark, but finally the kids said it was a place where they'd be safe from the rains. About that time Scott added that the Ark in the Bible could be viewed as a symbol for a safe place, a safe haven — exactly the point I was leading up to and hoping to elicit from the kids! Hopefully this discussion not only drew upon the kids' prior knowledge to relate the new to the known, but also piqued their curiosity about The Ark that Leonard is associated with.

The following rather lengthy excerpts dealing with the discussion of the first chapters of *Norby, the Mixed-up Robot* may help to clarify the kind of detailed, probing discussion that aids students in understanding complex concepts.

February 22

Today I began reading to the kids Isaac and Janet Asimov's *Norby, the Mixed-up Robot*. It takes a while to get into the story, and I was afraid I'd lose the kids in chapter one, but Scott and I decided to read the book anyway because of the fascinating scientific and social concepts it introduces, and the fact that it's a good adventure story.

Before I arrived, Scott had talked with the kids about Asimov: that he makes science interesting and entertaining, and that he's written lots of books for kids as well as adults. Scott also elicited from the kids what they knew about sleep-learning, which is relevant to the opening chapter.

I began by telling the kids I'm interested in and concerned about the effects of technology upon our future. What is technology? Computers, machines, microchips, etc., according to the kids. I added that technology is using science for practical purposes, creating man-made things. After giving an example of cars of the future that we'll be able to program to show our route from one location to another, I then asked: What is a robot? Various answers: a computer with arms, a person-like computer, something that can do anything a human can do only faster. Jeni disagreed with that statement from Matt, saying that computers can't do everything a human can do. I asked how robots are different from computers, and they gave appropriate answers: robots can move, you can carry them with you (I mentioned lap-top computers), they can talk (not all can, we agreed). I forgot to mention that some non-robot computers can also talk.

I then asked what they knew about *holograms*. One boy pointed to the hologram on the cover of *The Mirrorstone*, by Michael Palin, which I had brought. Someone else said that holograms looked like supernatural beings. I then asked who had been to Disney World. Most had! And sure enough, they remembered the holograms from the Haunted

House — ghostlike dancers in the ballroom, ghostlike companion in a "car."

Once we got into the book itself, I was less than pleased with how I handled the reading and discussion. Since the chapter was so long, I at first didn't stop and ask the kids to predict. They tended to become fidgety: to draw, write, look at other books, and so forth. (I later saw much the same response when Scott read them a long picture book.) This reaction might simply reflect their need to move physically, but at first my inclination was to try to finish the chapter as quickly as possible, because the kids looked bored. Instead, I soon realized, the kids needed to be more actively involved through discussion. Of course, I *know* that such engagement is crucial, so I was a little disappointed in myself for not involving them from the outset.

When I finally asked how Agent Gidlow might "tear Jeff apart," someone mentioned brainwashing. Again I didn't have the presence of mind to follow up. Fortunately Scott asked the kids how Gidlow might brainwash Jeff. As usual, many of the responses were quite sophisticated:

~ give Jeff a shot to make him tell the truth
~ suck out his mind and replace it
~ shine a bright light on him, and put a gun to his head
~ use Chinese water torture

Obviously these kids have been watching the same television shows I have!

I suggested that we might wait until the next chapter to find out what *hyperdrive* is, but Scott wisely engaged the kids in predicting what it might be. He started with the meanings of the word parts: *hyper* + *drive*. Not many kids thought it would be a means of powering a spacecraft; most thought in terms of a car or similar vehicle (obviously more familiar to them) which would go super-fast.

Beyond this point, I did a better job of getting the kids to predict and to justify/explain their predictions. For example, when Jeff's brother Fargo said "TGAF" and the Admiral asked what it meant, Jeff hesitated, then said, "The Girls Are Findable." I elicited from the kids the clues that TGAF didn't really mean what Jeff said it did. When we brainstormed for what it might mean, the best suggestion was "Things Get After Fargo." Great!

February 27

This time I did a much better job of involving the kids in discussion, though perhaps still not as good a job as I should have of asking questions that followed up on their responses.

We reviewed the characters, the initials TGAF, and what had happened so far. (Some kids had been absent when I started the story, but I would have done most of this reviewing anyway.) We also did a character map to review some of the major characteristics of the main characters.

Then I introduced concepts important to the chapter. First I mostly explained the concept of a *matter transmitter,* beginning by asking the kids who have watched *Star Trek* to explain how the characters are transported down to planets or to other ships. We explained this to the rest of the class, and then I indicated that the matter transmitter in this story is roughly the same: it transforms matter into radiation and then back again. I asked the kids how they would feel about traveling that way.

Then we discussed the concept of an *antigrav* device. I divided the word into *anti + grav(ity)* and elicited from them what they knew about the word parts. Some of the kids knew that *anti* means "against." We then discussed what an antigrav device might be.

Finally, I asked the students if they thought robots could feel emotions, and why or why not. Generally they thought not. I told them that Norby in this story can. I suggested that they listen carefully and try to remember as much as they could about Norby, because afterwards I would ask them to draw a picture of him in the center of a piece of paper and do a character map stemming outward from the picture.

Then I read them chapter two, "Choosing a Robot." We stopped to discuss ideas and make predictions, as appropriate. For example, we tried to decide where the Space Command was in relation to Earth, Mars and Luna, and I drew a picture on the board. Afterwards we brainstormed for characteristics that describe Norby. The kids reminded me that they were supposed to justify what they said about a character by referring to the text!

Not wanting to erase our earlier character map from the board, I crowded my map into about half the space and made a terrible mess: it didn't show relationships among the various characteristics. Finally, I erased the other half of the board and suggested that we start again by deciding what *different kinds* of characteristics we had accumulated — in other words, we categorized the information. I was impressed with the kids' categories:

~ how he looks
~ things he does
~ feelings
~ personality

When I questioned whether feelings and personality were very different, the kids concluded that feelings are internal to the person, while personality is external: how the person is perceived. Wow! And during the discussion Mike even suggested that Norby's label falling off of him might be a symbol for his new life!!

I asked the kids to do, overnight, a second semantic map on Norby, this time with the details organized into the categories we'd brainstormed.

These examples show that even an experienced teacher can underestimate the extent and depth of discussion needed to help students gain as much as possible from a text. They also show how I continued learning from my own experience and Scott's example, and how I reflected upon my experiences in order to guide discussion more effectively in the future. These, too, are characteristics of whole language teachers.

Assessment and evaluation

In the classrooms of experienced whole language teachers, assessment (the gathering of data) and evaluation include:

~ teacher evaluation of students
~ student and teacher self-evaluation
~ student and teacher evaluation of the curriculum as it has emerged through negotiation

Since our evaluation of ourselves as teachers permeates much of what we have already written in this chapter, the following discussion focuses primarily on the other aspects of evaluation.

Teacher evaluation of students

Fortunately we remembered to engage the students in self-evaluation and evaluation of the overall learning experience as the group projects were being brought to fruition. However, we did little in the way of recording data for evaluating individual students, for several reasons:

~ We were reluctant to evaluate *them* when we were doing so much experimenting with our own teaching.

~ In the daily flow of our projects we didn't have much time to write down our observations.

~ At the outset of the project we weren't able to foresee which factors we would want to assess the students on.

~ We were so involved in our role as collaborators that the usual role of teacher as evaluator paled in significance.

In many ways, evaluation seemed much less important than the learning we witnessed daily. Whatever records we did keep took the form of journal comments over time. Take, for example, Connie's reflections on Brian's growth.

April 12

The group dynamics during this discussion [on how to divide the writing of the play] were interesting. Every other time when we'd gathered our chairs in a group, Brian was among the last to arrive. (He always took a bathroom break with the class, whereas many of the others in the group didn't.) Therefore, he always seemed to get a chair at the outer edge of a semicircle (where it was difficult to see the TV screen for a videotape) or in the back row.

I had tried shuffling chairs before, but today I insisted that we enlarge our circle to get Brian (and I think, Jill) into the main circle. And by golly, he actually volunteered a couple of suggestions. For the first time, he came alive in the group. . . .

Some of the kids wanted to get started writing the play immediately and suggested that they come in after lunch to do so. They talked me into eating lunch with them. (Ugh! The kinds of food are much more interesting than in my school days, but the food isn't much better tasting!) Then after lunch, Amanda, Brandy, Melissa and — surprise! — Brian returned to the classroom to work on the play. . . .

The three girls wanted to practice scene two, in which the drug dealers try to sell drugs to the children on the playground. . . . Brian and Melissa tried playing the role of the two abused sisters, while Amanda and Brandy were the drug dealers. I was pleased to see Brian so involved with the others in trying to write the scene by walking and talking their way through it — especially since he won't even have a part in this scene.

April 24

The day Brian finally began speaking up in the group and actually gave up noon recess to act/write with the girls was the first time I saw him look really alive. This has continued through the writing of the play. He types fairly rapidly and has really begun to enjoy composing. His sense of humor — which I suspect his classmates and teacher rarely see in school — has also begun to emerge. For example, he and Jeni got into a discussion the next time we met in the computer lab about how their scene of the parents fighting should be "rated." R? PG-13? X? His humor also comes through in some of his word choices: "clunker" for the parents' old car, "brats" for the two kids, and so forth. He seems to enjoy thinking of just the right word.

April 30-May 2

. . . Brian and Jeni (the father and mother in the play) worked well together. They seemed to appreciate each other's humor and really enjoyed writing, especially the fight scene. They did a great job of it, too. Occasionally they'd jab or slap each other playfully, but it seemed to be just that: good-natured bantering.

May 31

Jenny and Brian became especially good at conveying emotions through facial expressions. . . .

As part of the students' self-evaluation and evaluation of the project, Brian described his involvement in his own words:

> I liked a lot of things during the time limit that I was in the social group, like practicing the play in the cafeteria and doing the play. I learned a lot just by watching one movie. I learned a lot about drugs and how to say no as many times as possible to get away from them. I like watching the play on tape.

About halfway through the project, Scott commented that he thought he'd never seen as passive a student as Brian in his fifteen years of teaching. It was especially gratifying, then, that Brian came alive and participated so enthusiastically in writing and acting the play. Two assessments by Connie seem particularly pertinent:

> I should have made more of an effort sooner to get Brian into the circle of discussants — though at least he apparently did learn from the videotape that I feared he could scarcely see.

> Brian's ultimate excitement about the project clearly reveals the value of encouraging students to choose many of their own learning experiences — the things they are interested in. Previously passive students like Brian may become involved and enthusiastic learners when allowed to make significant decisions about what and how they will learn.

Our evaluation of student progress was informal in that no formal pre- or post-testing was incorporated into the project. However, our informal observations and journal entries allowed us to see aspects of the students that normally wouldn't be included in evaluation, when assessment is limited to traditional testing and grades. Connie's comments about Brian, for example, give a more textured, detailed view of his development than a test score or daily-work average could ever give.

Our concern, then, is not with the type of evaluation we used. It's that we didn't set up a systematic, organized way of gathering information about the students. Our approach was simply too "hit and miss" to be truly effective. The next time we engage in such a project we'd like to keep a portfolio for each student, a file that would include:

~ systematic as well as anecdotal teacher observations;
~ student surveys and responses to questions or questionnaires;
~ representative samples of student work;
~ student self-evaluation.

We would also begin each class by asking the students what they intend to work on that day, and if they have everything they need to do so — in other words, to start with a "state of the class" conference like those Atwell describes in *In the Middle*. Having the students record each day what they did at home in preparation for that day's class, and having them evaluate themselves for their efforts, seems another excellent strategy. It might not only help them to assess their work, but also stimulate them to take more initiative outside of class than some of our students did.

Teacher observations need to be recorded not only anecdotally, when something especially interesting happens, but systematically as well. For example, we'd concentrate on two or three students each day, for a specified number of days each week. We now realize that from such informal records we might have compiled a summary sheet for each student on factors like the following, all with emphasis on the student's *growth*:

~ how much preparation the student typically did outside of class (from the "state of the class" conferences or the student's daily records);
~ how well the student typically used class time;
~ how well the student worked with others;
~ how well the student seemed to grasp the materials and concepts dealt with;
~ the quality of the "products" the student produced.

As the next section will suggest, however, ongoing student self-evaluation is probably more important than evaluation by the teacher. At the very least, final evaluation should be negotiated between teacher and student, the two conferring over a summary sheet prepared by the teacher and a similar summary sheet completed by the student. Ideally, the students should know in advance the factors that will enter into evaluation. The following is an example of a summary evaluation form. In actual practice the form would require both sides of a single sheet, leaving room for both descriptive and evaluative comments.

Name _____ Date_____

Effort outside of class:

Use of class time:

Working with others:

Understanding of material:

Project(s):

SUMMARY:

Adequate assessment of student participation in a collaborative project is a need that clearly emerged from our theme exploration. On the other hand, we must admit that in the excitement of learning together, assessment didn't seem very important. We wouldn't want to become so obsessed with assessment and evaluation as to destroy the collaborative spirit of such a project.

Student self-evaluation

Although Connie made an aborted attempt to have the students assess their work periodically by asking her social concerns students to jot on index cards what they'd done in preparation for each class, and Scott often reminded the students in the environment group to describe in their journal what they were doing, it was only at the end of the project that the children were encouraged to engage in reflective self-evaluation.

Because working collaboratively was one of the new and distinctive features of this project, we had decided to focus the students' attention on how well the groups worked together. Scott led the class in a discussion of some of their individual strengths and thoughts for improvement, then asked them to write a paragraph in response to the following questions: What did you learn about your particular strengths as a group member? What might you need to work on? He deliberately tried to focus their attention on how they might do better in the future, rather than on castigating themselves for perceived weaknesses.

The students seemed refreshingly honest in their responses — due, we think, to the climate of trust that had been established both before and during the theme exploration project. Several of the students commented on how well, or how inappropriately, they worked with others. The following are examples:

> I think my strength was helping people out like if they were having trouble writing a report I would help them and give them ideas. I think I need to work on supporting my answers. I think that because my answers are never good.

> I learned my strengths were helping others do their work, finding information, doing reports. I need work on taking notes and not bossing people.

> What I need to work on is more cooperation, because in our group we have a majority and lots of time I got out voted and complained because nobody did it my way.

> I think I need to improve on listening to other people and their ideas. I also need to cooperate with other people.

> If someone needed something such as tape, the stapler, tacks, paper, or any other things I'd go look for it. I also needed to work on something: complaining. If I had to write a report I'd try to get out of it some way. I never did.

Although several students thought one of their strengths was their willingness and ability to work with and help their groupmates, self-criticism in the area of cooperation was frequent. Other students emphasized strengths like working alone, recopying reports, acting, finding something else to do after finishing one task, learning from the materials they read.

Perhaps the most poignant self-evaluative comment was written in response to a question about what they liked least about the project:

> The thing I liked the least was when I was trying to run the whole play. Now when I look back at the days I did that, I feel so, so, so stupid.

With students demonstrating insights like this, teacher evaluation seems almost an unnecessary insult. We only wish that we had engaged the students in self-evaluation earlier in the project, so that they could have worked on what they perceived as areas for improvement.

Student evaluation of the project

During the last week of classes, we spent considerable time engaging the students in evaluating the project. The essence of our discussion is captured in Connie's journal entry:

June 1

Scott began by reminding the kids that the kinds of projects we'd been working on weren't the kinds they'd ordinarily do in a language arts class. What would they usually do? The kids listed some activities — spelling, grammar, etc. In this case we were doing social studies and science, with language arts facilitating our explorations (that's my phrasing, of course, not theirs). Since the environmental group and the technology group had both dealt at least in part with science, Scott engaged the kids in brainstorming on the differences between how science is usually taught and how it was explored in the project. . . .

Scott recorded the ideas in a semantic map, using the overhead. Because the map quickly became messy, I've incorporated the ideas into the following lists, using as much of the original wording as I could record:

What would be done in a typical science class	What we did in this class
Use single text.	No text. Everyone reads something different. Use magazines, posters, etc.
Work by yourself.	Team work.
Usually teacher picks/assigns topic and tells you who to work with.	Choose own group, by topic. Choose own subtopic within the group, and choose who to work with.
Usually watch while teacher makes things, does experiments. Or the teacher tells you what to do.	Teacher mainly provides materials that the student wants/needs to make things or do experiments. (You get help to do things yourself, instead of watching the teacher.)
You just sit there and go over stuff you already know.	It's funner. You choose what to do and usually choose something new.
You do dittos.	You write your own reports.
You're told what you *have* to do.	You learn what you *want* to know.
	You study things that will help you in the future; things that will help you when you get older.
	You choose what you will do; you don't have people looking over your shoulder.
	They trust you when you're on your own.
Write a report. And/or do a ditto, take a test.	Do final project. It makes you more confident.
Read one chapter after another.	Set your own order.
Science out of a book — you're just reading it.	On your own — nobody to go to, more responsibility.

After these lists had been compiled through group discussion, Scott then asked the students to write responses to these questions:

~ What did you like best about this project? Why?

~ What did you like least about the project? Why?

~ Which do you like better, the way things are done in a traditional science (or other) class, or the way we did them in this language arts class?

~ What is the most important thing you learned about your subject — and why is it important? (He told them they could list more than one important thing.)

~ What did you learn about your strengths as a group member? What might you need to work on?

In response to the question about which approach they preferred, *all* of the students preferred the approach used during this project, and for many of the same reasons as the group had previously brainstormed. A major reason was that they find the texts, the assignments and the sheer repetitive nature of traditional teaching boring. In contrast, our theme exploration was more fun and more exciting because it allowed them to work on something that interested them, that they enjoyed.

Another major factor was that they had more freedom to make decisions: to choose their group by topic, to choose the particular subtopic they would work on, to choose the classmates they would work with. They appreciated the opportunity to work actively and independent of constant teacher direction. They also valued being able to work with other students — offering and seeking help, or just working collaboratively and companionably.

What follows is a representative sample of the students' responses, some from each of the three groups:

> I liked it the way we did it because you got to pick your own subject. I also liked it because I learned what I wanted to learn about and I didn't have to learn something boring that doesn't interest me very much. I also liked it this way

because I had fun and with a text book I usually don't have fun. But this way you did experiments and had fun with your friends. Maybe what I learned will help us in the future.

Caryn, environmental group

I liked the way we did it because I hate using text books, because you have to read the same thing at the same time. I liked the way we did it because we can study what we want to with partners, so if you get lost and don't understand something they can help you.

Heather, environmental group

I liked the way we did it in L.A. because you don't feel like you're going to fall asleep. It's a lot funner. You do fun experiments, like you see what happens with oil spills, try to clean it up, you see what carbon is, you see what acid rain does, and lots of other things. The traditional way just reads the book and does dittos.

Anna, environmental group

I like the new way because you are more on your own. For example in homeroom you get out books and go over stuff you already know. In here you learn new things about planes and cars. Like I said to Mr. Peterson, you're more on your own.

Jerome, technology group

I liked the way we did it in L.A. because it was more fun and exciting than the traditional way. The reason it's more fun is because you're with a partner and you're discussing things with your partner.

Andrew, technology group

I liked the way we did it because we were more independent. Nobody was telling us what to do, we could do it the way we chose. I like it better this way because we can do what we want and nobody was looking over our shoulder but just enough guidance so we're not on our own, but you're not telling us what to do.

Brandy, social concerns group

I liked our way because we're free — we can pick our books that we want to read, that has to do with our group name. We don't do everything the same. We read all different books, not just one book for each person in a class. In our group, we do plays, paragraphs and stories. In the other way we do worksheets and dittos.

Brian, social concerns group

These and similar comments clarify why students prefer what we know as a whole language approach to learning and teaching.

The things they liked least were much more diverse than those they liked best. The most frequent complaint was difficulty working with their partner. The second most frequent complaint had to do with the work involved: "research was long and hard," as one student put it, and others apparently found writing reports to be tedious. Some students didn't like doing reports while others (the environment group) were doing experiments, and still others (the social concerns group) were watching movies and working in the computer lab. Concerns expressed by one or two students included the difficulty of finding good information on their topic, the depressing nature of their topic (this from students in both the environment group and the social concerns group), and not having enough time to do things perfectly. Two students were particularly dissatisfied with their costumes for the play!

On the whole, it was interesting, but not surprising, that working cooperatively with other students was both one of the most positive things and one of the most negative things about the project. Most students enjoyed taking more responsibility and working more independently, but one student in the technology group (which received less adult help at first) pinpointed this as what he liked least about the project. Indeed, even the students who clearly preferred independence, both in making decisions about what they would study and with whom and in carrying out the details of their projects, still wanted their teacher to guide, facilitate and sometimes collaborate with them on their work.

Final reflections on our goals

As the following comments testify, we both made significant progress toward achieving our personal goals as teachers, both during the project and afterwards as we continued to reflect upon it.

Connie

Regarding my own growth as a teacher during this project, I feel that I made significant progress in allowing and encouraging student ownership of learning while still facilitating their learning through my role as teacher. The interesting thing is that before engaging in this project I sometimes conceptualized negotiating the curriculum as a matter of sharing control with students. During the project, however, I never once asked myself "Who is in control here?" or "Who should have control?" The issue of control simply disappeared as we worked collaboratively together.

Scott

Through this project, I met my goal of creating a learning environment that was both personally meaningful and specifically relevant to life outside the classroom. One recurring theme in the students' evaluations of the project was the importance of being able to choose topics and projects that were meaningful. As one student said, she felt "grown-up" because she had control over her own learning. My feeling that freedom and responsibility would lift students' eyes beyond the classroom to the outside world was also reinforced. I felt I'd reached my goal when one student closed his evaluation of the project with this statement, "Now I know what to expect in the future."

Final reflections on the project

Doubters may say it's all well and good that the students generally liked this approach better than a more traditional approach — but did they learn as much?

There is no simple answer. The students in the environment group probably learned more information than they would have in traditional study, because they were actively involved in doing experiments and researching their topics. The students in the technology group may have learned less than they might otherwise have learned in the same amount of time, because they focused their attention so narrowly on cars and planes of the future. The students in the social concerns group learned some about child abuse and a lot about saying no to drugs, but would have at least been *exposed* to more factual information in the same amount of time in a more traditional classroom. If learning is measured as factual information that can be readily taught and tested (and soon forgotten!), then the students in one or two of the groups may have "learned" less than they would have through conventional teaching.

However, whole language teachers strongly resist this concept of learning. They believe that the attitudes, skills and values students develop are, in the long run, far more important than any particular facts they may or may not have mastered. Our students' concern for the future of our environment, their interest in the technology of the future, their desire to help solve social problems will endure long after the factual information has been forgotten. In becoming eager and independent learners, they have increased their likelihood of becoming lifelong learners. In learning how to work more cooperatively to solve problems, they have begun to develop a skill crucial to the survival of our world. To whole language teachers, developing such attitudes, skills and values is far more important than mastering isolated facts.

Connie

In reflecting on what we did and didn't accomplish during our theme exploration, I realized that, as always, there was something lost as well as something gained: every decision to do one thing entailed a decision not to do lots of others. I particularly regret not having time to engage in ongoing assessment with the students, or to continue the literature discussions on *Cracker Jackson,* or to help the students learn editing skills and experience the editing of their own work.

For a while I really struggled with the fact that the "product" my group produced, the play, came to take precedence over so many significant processes. It bothered me that we had to ignore so many opportunities for learning because we had deadlines for writing, rehearsing and producing the play. I began to wonder if we could legitimately call our project "theme exploration."

Eventually, though, I concluded that what the children learned in writing and producing the play was as valuable as what they might have learned by dealing more thoroughly with "content." One of the things they obviously learned was that doing something in a professional manner requires time, effort and dedication. As a result of the effort they devoted to the play, I think they finished the project with a sense of pride for the professional job they had done, and a sense, too, that the videotape might actually help someone when it was aired on cable TV. These affective results may be far more lasting and valuable than anything the students may or may not have learned in the way of factual information, or even of writing skills.

Over the course of a year, it would be important to balance the kinds of theme explorations and projects to be undertaken. A theme heavily involving science should be balanced by one emphasizing social studies, for instance. A literature theme on a topic could be balanced by another on a genre, and still another on a particular author. The experience of writing a play could be balanced by experience in doing experiments, in doing research and writing reports, and so forth. Collaboratively, the teacher and students could decide on a series of themes that would offer the class a variety of learning experiences and that, together, would not only expose the students to factual information but help them develop as fully functioning human beings and fully contributing members of society.

Scott

Exploring a theme with students is at times a scary and risky business. As a teacher, you wander into a forest without the security of a curriculum guide to lead you between and among the trees. Consequently, the kids don't progress in a straight line from point A to point B, nor do you go home every night with a stack of dittos under your arm to reassure yourself that you accomplished something that day. There is, to say the least, no little uncertainty in an undertaking like this, as this comment from my journal points out:

April 16

Sometimes my room seems like a train station. People hustling about, some standing in corners talking, others sprawled in chairs discussing heaven knows what, adults coming in and going out. It certainly doesn't look like a traditional classroom, with a teacher standing at the head of the class and kids quietly pushing pencils across paper. Point to consider: Is this the most efficient way to learn? Is this *any* way to learn?

The answer to these questions is that thematic teaching may not be the most efficient way of teaching, but it certainly is an effective way of learning. Teaching such a "unit" is not a neat, tidy job. When you let students negotiate the curriculum and choose the paths they wish to follow, things do not stay within the tidy boundaries of a packaged curriculum. But, on the other hand, learning goes well beyond the mere compiling of facts. In a thematic unit, learning becomes deeper and more profound; it wanders outside the narrow confines of the classroom and into the world; and it is better able to withstand the witherings of time.

Recently, as I was browsing in a local bookstore, a parent of a student from last year's class stopped me: the class in which we undertook theme exploration. This was at the peak of the Gulf War and thousands of gallons of oil were spilling into the Persian Gulf at the very moment we were talking. Her son, the woman told me, was extremely concerned about the environmental catastrophe. He remembered the experiments the environment group had done with the oil bowl — the thick, heavy smell of crude oil floating on water — and how difficult it was to clean the oil off the rocks and out of the water. He was concerned, she told me, that the damage done by this one act alone would last far beyond the end of the war.

To me, this two-minute conversation in a crowded retail store demonstrated the power of theme exploration far better than any objective test could ever measure. My former student had carried the knowledge acquired from the experiment far beyond the boundaries of the classroom and applied it to the world. It had developed in him a social conscience and a budding awareness of the world outside his immediate environment.

~ ~ ~ ~ ~ ~ ~ ~ ~ ~ ~ ~ ~

Whole language principles in action: First-grade retrospect

~ ~ ~ ~ ~ ~

Joel

Both Connie and I have long admired *A Ring of Endless Light* by Madeleine L'Engle, the third in her series about Vicky Austin and her family. Towards the end of the novel, Vicky has a long conversation with her friend, Adam, a young scientist helping with research on dolphin communication. Adam tells Vicky he admires a poem she has written because it exhibits her "archaic understanding": that is, her "understanding of things in their deepest, mythic sense." He, on the other hand, is pulled by "the Cartesian world" which, he tells her, "insists on keeping intellectual control, and that means you have to let go your archaic understanding, because that means going along with all kinds of things you can't control." (pp.239-40) Adam goes on to praise the fact that Vicky can work with others. He explains: "A lot of discoveries come through teamwork, with two completely different types of imagination working together and being far more than either one alone." (p.241)

Adam's words serve to articulate two of the most important principles we had as goals for our first-grade project: to relinquish control and promote collaboration.

Letting students take control and creating a community of readers and writers seemed nearly impossible at the beginning of the project, but in the end we were at least moderately successful in practicing some of the whole language principles we claimed to espouse in chapter two. The point is, we articulated those principles long after we had finished the project. In fact, I never consciously thought about the weather unit in terms of specific whole language principles until after we had completed it.

As in the preceding chapter, there is some overlapping of categories in what follows. It is difficult to discuss learners, curriculum and the teacher's role separately.

Learning and the learner

For me, the first-grade project had a number of personal and professional learning goals:

- ~ I was concerned with helping students on their journey towards becoming lifelong learners and lifetime readers and writers.
- ~ Having little experience with this age group, I was personally interested in seeing how children this young would tackle a theme project.
- ~ I was used to a transmission model of teaching, and I hoped the project would help me shift towards transactional learning.
- ~ I wanted to be sure the students felt that what they were learning was both functional and purposeful.
- ~ I wanted to create a learning environment in which risks were rewarded.

Transactional learning

Earlier we stated that significant and enduring learning is transactional. In working with the first-graders, Nora, Vickie and I tried to ensure that the children constantly interacted with us and with each other, as well as with printed matter. Although we spent a lot of time in large groups, the children often collaborated in small groups to read to each other and work on projects, as when they flew paper airplanes and made cloud pictures. Virtually every time they wrote, they shared their stories with at least part of the group.

In encouraging the children to write, we tried to steer them away from mere "sentences" and "paragraphs" towards letters, newspaper articles, stories, poems and other authentic forms of writing. Editing became important because they were "publishing" their work in a class magazine. They created a poster of the water-cycle so they could teach the concept to another class of first-graders.

The same held true for reading. They never opened their basal readers once during their "weather" time. Instead, they read trade books and magazines — the kind they could find in their own libraries. They watched an episode of *Reading Rainbow,* a real television series — real in the sense that they could watch it in their homes as well as at school.

Of course, the subject of the project was also very real. Each day the children were being affected by weather somehow, as when they had to miss recess because the playground was too muddy. All of them had experienced rain, snow, wind and hail, and many had seen tornados. Even the guest weather forecaster was someone they already knew — he had visited the year before and was a neighbor to some of them.

The project provided the children with many opportunities to make meaning of their world. There is usually a "manufactured" quality to thematic units, but we tried to make ours less artificial. This is not to say that we avoided the transmission model of learning entirely. There were times, as when we instructed the children in the wonders of rainmaking, the water cycle and the genesis of a thunderstorm, that I felt as if we were lecturing to them. They never had to memorize facts, however, and we always tried to provide them with a real context for whatever we were discussing. Moreover, learning wasn't competitive. We worked together, brainstormed, encouraged each other, always clapped when someone shared a piece of writing — in short, made discoveries through teamwork, as L'Engle's Adam Eddington suggests in the quote at the beginning of this chapter.

Functional and purposeful learning

I suppose I shouldn't have been surprised when the students seemed more interested in how to play with snow than in why it snows. For them, the technical aspects of weather did not, at first, seem either purposeful or functional. When I teach composition, I tell my students to ask one important question each time they write something: who cares? The first-graders asked the same question with their eyes each time we delved into the scientific.

We were most successful with our scientific discussions when the children saw a purpose in them, so we talked about those aspects of weather that seemed functional and important, like what to do when it rains or snows. When we talked about tornados, the children were quite interested in how they develop, recognizing that knowing that might help them tell when one is approaching. They were attentive when I shared Franklyn Branley's *Tornado Alert* because it told them how to protect themselves.

The writing they did was also functional. Although we engaged in little direct discussion of the mechanics of writing, when the students wrote letters, they were very concerned about how to begin and end them. When it came time to edit the classroom magazine, they became more interested in spelling and punctuation. At that point, they were willing to learn some of the rules that real writers follow.

An environment that encourages risk-taking

Few classes could have been better prepared for this kind of project than Nora's. The children had been reading and writing since September, and they regularly shared their work. Even so, when I first arrived in their classroom I had to convince them that I, too, would give them positive rather than negative feedback. The first day I worked with them, they were very concerned about how to spell every word in their stories about snowstorms. They had already become comfortable with inventive spelling, but suddenly they were worrying about correctness. Once they were reassured that I also accepted inventive spellings, they went to work with amazing speed.

At first they wanted constant reassurance that, if they chose to write in a form I had modeled, they were doing it the "right" way. Most of them soon became comfortable with me, convinced that they could take risks with me as they did with Nora, but I had to keep reassuring a few, throughout the project, that there was room for error — I guess they wanted to see if I had changed my mind. (This need for reassurance also manifested itself in their desire for attention. A child would feel hurt if his or her idea was not heard, despite the fact that 20 other children had voiced theirs. And each day when I came to class at least one child wanted to give me a present, ranging from pencils to valentines to paper airplanes.)

Ironically, the children themselves were much quicker to find fault than were the teachers. They regularly corrected each other's mistakes, and in some cases a positive comment from one of the teachers would be needed to overcome peer criticism.

However, in some ways it was the adults who were most concerned about taking risks. I worried both about losing control of the classroom and about not dazzling Nora and Vickie with my teaching techniques. Coming into a first-grade classroom with very little experience at that level and trying to practice whole language principles when I was still learning what whole language *was* also entailed risk. Nora openly admitted to feeling uncomfortable teaching music and poetry writing. I suspect that she also wondered whether I approved of what she did in the classroom, although I tried to reassure her. Vickie, who taught a wonderful lesson on clouds, admitted afterwards that she was frightened to death to teach in front of Nora and me.

In practice, Nora was quite good at supporting what the students did. She would ask the students questions to help them examine their ideas and thoughts, but she never told them they were wrong. If necessary, she would pose another question. She would also entertain any ideas the students had when they brainstormed. I found myself trying to emulate her. When the students brainstormed ways to make it rain, I was open to pouring Koolaid into the clouds and to throwing one's dog or sister into the air to make a hole in a rain cloud — two answers that seemed illogical and silly at first.

When the children wrote poems, I tried to reduce the risk by having the class provide ideas and words that anyone could borrow. I also suggested different ways they might shape a poem and gave them a model they might follow for help. I emphasized that these directions were not requirements, that they were simply intended to help give the children confidence that they, too, could write poetry. Some children risked moving beyond the words the class had chosen; others remained heavily influenced by the class discussion, but still produced poems that pleased them and made them feel like real writers.

The chaos of learning

We also stated earlier that learners develop at their own pace, and that learning is idiosyncratic, unpredictable, chaotic. Our project certainly made this clear to me. Every one of Nora's students seemed to be at a different level in their ability to read and write. Often the writing of one ESL student from India was a mish-mash of words that made little sense and had nothing to do with what we had been discussing. Another boy was excelling if he produced a single sentence on a subject, or even a couple of words. On the other hand, several children wrote eloquent and creative stories and verses. One girl produced two or three pages every time she wrote.

Sometimes it was difficult to help the students. The three of us would wander through the class, beset by dozens of children wanting immediate responses to what they had written and needing various kinds of help. Perhaps the most important thing we did was to encourage them and praise their efforts, no matter what level they were at. This doesn't mean that we didn't ask them questions, or encourage them to look again at what they had done. The emphasis, however, was not on product. The mere fact that they were reading, writing and thinking about weather was the important thing.

Social collaboration

The children had ample opportunity to work together. Virtually every session involved some sort of brainstorming: coming up with "rain" words, deciding how evaporation works, fantasizing about why it thunders, sharing weather-forecasting tips. A good part of their collaboration, however, occurred outside of the more structured class sessions.

I will always remember how surprised I was to see the children teaching each other to read on my first visit to the class. I knew it was possible; I just wasn't sure that I really believed it was practical. They would get into small groups of three or four and share books with one another. If they didn't know a word, others in the group would help them.

Nora had already provided the framework for collaborative writing as well. When they wrote they sometimes helped each other with ideas or spellings and they often read what they had written to others. This sort of collaboration continued throughout the project.

Nature and development of the curriculum

My initial interest in the project had to do with curriculum development, at least partly because of my love of children's literature. Certainly this aspect of the project was enjoyable. At the same time, however, I learned some important things about negotiating the curriculum and teaching skills in context. As the project progressed, I became increasingly aware that the curriculum should be for the students, not the students for the curriculum.

Literature and other reading materials

Nora's students were excited about reading and had frequent opportunities to choose their own books and share them with each other. Early in the project we decided that we needed to create a classroom library of books on weather. The children were still only beginning to learn how to use the school library and we needed materials we could leave in Nora's room. Since I was also convinced that we ought to emphasize literature in the large-group discussions, it was even more important to find appropriate books on our subject.

We had several concerns. First, we needed to provide a *variety* of materials. Not all students would be interested in the same aspects of weather and we needed to give them the chance to make some choices. We would have to find books about snow, rain, wind, severe weather, clouds, forecasting, etc. We would also have to look for books from a variety of genres: fiction (fantasy, realistic fiction, folktales, historical fiction), non-fiction and poetry. We would also need books of varying difficulty. While most of the children could read quite well, a few could not.

It was also important to find books that would *appeal* to the children and present ideas in ways that would be *appropriate* for their level of development. I spent time ensuring that our library included works of high literary and artistic quality, but we never pushed "high quality" books on the children during their free reading. While I have long promoted using quality literature with children, I feel there is value in virtually anything that will get a child to read. I used to read popular series books such as the Hardy Boys and comic books of all sorts. I also read virtually every book that had won the Newbery Award. What mattered to me as a young reader was whether or not a book addressed my interests, concerns and problems. We especially tried to find books with young protagonists — like Keats' *The Snowy Day* and Gundersheimer's *Happy Winter* — that look at weather from the point of view of a young child.

Finding materials was actually very easy. To begin with, "weather" is a fairly broad topic that has been dealt with in a variety of books. My first step was simply consulting the computerized card catalog of the children's section of the Springfield Public library. I browsed through the "weather" section, and within a short time I became acquainted with a number of suitable titles. I was intrigued, for example, by the bizarre anecdotes about weather in Franklyn Branley's *It's Raining Cats and Dogs: All Kinds of Weather and Why We Have It.* The powerful photographs in Seymour Simon's *Storms* are enough to leave anyone with a healthy respect for tornados and hurricanes. Valerie Wyatt's *Weather Watch* was an education in itself. (Did you know that a hailstone bigger than a grapefruit hit the town of Potter, Nebraska, on July 6, 1928?)

Since I wanted to locate a variety of materials, however, I continued my search, consulting some standard bibliographies of children's books. The NCTE publication by Mary Jett-Simpson, *Adventuring With Books*, includes some subject bibliographies ("Earth Science, Meteorology, and Oceanography," for instance) and a helpful topical index. Like most bibliographies, unfortunately, it has its limitations. The newest edition annotates only books published between 1985 and 1989, although it also includes a general non-annotated list of earlier books.

Other useful bibliographies include *Science Books for Children* (Wilms), Bowker's annual *Subject Guide to Children's Books in Print* and *A to Zoo: Subject Access to Children's Picture Books* (Lima). Some of the children's books I found, such as Caroline Bauer's *Snowy Day: Stories and Poems*, also include bibliographies of related materials. A mini-bibliography of aids for selecting children's books appears on pages 193-195.

I found that I had to make a conscious effort to seek out children's fiction and poetry, since they aren't always included in the bibliographies. I spent one afternoon browsing through the picture books in the curriculum library at Southwest Missouri State University and was amply rewarded.

People, too, were great resources. Nora approached her school librarian, who pulled from the shelves a number of books on weather. Virginia Gleason of the Springfield Public Library and Jeanne Walsh of the Book Nook were both very helpful. And because I try to keep up with new children's books and have a longstanding interest in books about winter myself, I already knew of a few titles I wanted to use.

In the end we had more material than the children could ever hope to use. So I began the process of sifting through it, looking specifically for books that were readable, well written and relevant to first-graders. While I didn't consciously think about it at the time, I realize that I employed some fairly simple criteria in choosing books for the project. Some of these appear in Appendix 3, pages 222-224.

By pooling books from the Springfield Public Library, the Ezard Elementary School library, Nora's classroom and my own personal collection, we developed a core of over 100 titles, which we supplemented with miscellaneous magazines. Many of these became the focus of group discussions. When they were not in use, we merely heaped them on a table in the back of the classroom where the children could choose whatever interested them. The books we read aloud to the class became the most popular, but during the project the students read from many of the other books as well, frequently gravitating to those that tell a distinct story or that are fanciful or humorous.

In the end, we managed to provide the children with a wide variety of weather books worthy of their time and interest, as the following categories and examples show:

- ~ fantasy: Judi Barrett's *Cloudy With a Chance of Meatballs*;
- ~ realistic fiction: Ezra Jack Keats' *The Snowy Day*;

- folktales: Verna Aardema's *Bringing the Rain to Kapiti Plain*;
- biography: Peter and Connie Roop's *Keep the Lights Burning, Abbie*;
- poetry: Jack Prelutsky's *It's Snowing! It's Snowing!*

We included books that focused on weather in a variety of ways:

- Seymour Simon's *Storms* contains visually interesting pictures;
- Valerie Wyatt's *Weather Watch* includes science projects children can do on their own;
- Robert McCloskey's *Time of Wonder* describes a family bonding together during a hurricane;
- Karen Gundersheimer's *Happy Winter* is an indoor version of *The Snowy Day*;
- Mary Stolz's *Storm in the Night* is about a boy and his grandfather who tell stories to pass the time during a thunderstorm;
- Charlotte Zolotow's *The Storm Book* details a wild storm.

The collection also contained many informational books, like the recently reissued series by Franklyn Branley (*Air Is All Around You; Flash, Crash, Rumble, and Roll; Hurricane Watch; Snow Is Falling; Tornado Alert*) that details various kinds of weather. Among other things, they incorporate simple scientific explanations for certain kinds of weather, safety precautions children might take, and an assortment of interesting weather facts.

Appendix 3 includes a sample, annotated bibliography of books relating to snow and winter (pages 224-230). There's nothing special about those books, but they illustrate the diversity of titles the students were able to choose from.

It's difficult to tell how many of them the children actually read, since I wasn't with them during much of their free-reading time. But on each visit I snooped around their desks and found that they were choosing books about weather along with others they were reading. And at various times during the project I recall children reading some of them to me.

Negotiating the curriculum

In the preceding chapter, Connie and Scott pointed out that "negotiating the curriculum" is an unfortunate phrase, since it suggests that teachers and students are adversaries. For Nora, Vickie and me, the phrase came to mean providing the students with choices.

As we began the project, we brainstormed with the children for potential topics relating to a study of the weather, thus allowing them to help shape what followed. We started out feeling it was important for the class to learn about some of the scientific aspects of weather, experiment with many forms of writing and experience a variety of books about weather. But we altered our plans to fit what the children seemed to want, emphasizing how weather affected them personally, reading fictional stories related to weather, and writing about their feelings and personal experiences. A weather change quickly made us shift from talking about snow to reading and writing about rain, because it was of more immediate interest to the children. We talked about thunder in the context of the children's fears and introduced clouds by discussing images they had seen in the sky. In essence, our curriculum derived from their interests.

We also tried to provide the children with choices each day. They could choose which books they would read — or if they would even read about weather. When we wrote, we developed possible writing projects as a group (rain poems, stories about severe weather, "pourquoi" tales about rainbows and rainmaking), but the children could write about other topics or in other forms if they preferred.

When I first visited Conway, I was impressed by the kinds of choices Nora allowed her students to make. After we finished the project, I interviewed Vickie about Nora and her class. Vickie detailed the rigid nature of the district-imposed curriculum and praised the freedom Nora gives her students. She also felt that, by casting them in the role of teachers, Nora allowed the children to help develop the curriculum for each other. What follows is an excerpt from my interview with Vickie:

Joel: Do you feel that Nora allows her students to negotiate their own curriculum?

Vickie: Oh, yes. She gives them choices all the time. I've heard her say thousands and thousands of times, "You may read a story in your reading book, you may choose a story from the back of the classroom, you may write a story about anything to do with what we have studied about" — all kinds of choices.

If children choose an outside reading book, they find out how many words they can read in it. They might not be able to read but one or two words in the book. Nora and I sit down next to them and work with them. I take half the class and she takes the other half. The children show us in their books how many words they can read. They get praise if they can read two words and, of course, as the year progresses, they read more and more words, until finally they are reading whole books. They have a goal — if they can read a library book all the way through, they get to read it to the kindergarten.

Joel: So they become teachers.

Vickie: Sure. They become teachers. They also become peer tutors. They read to each other.

The following excerpt from my journal, reiterates what Vickie said about Nora:

January 29

I have been very concerned about how to help Nora's students become more independent. I suppose that, as someone who likes to have control of the classroom when I'm teaching, I have a lot to learn. I probably shouldn't worry, though. Today I observed Nora working with her students, teaching them about money. I suppose, like some teachers I've seen, she might have created a ditto with a number of story problems. Instead, after taking suggestions from the class, she pretended that they were attending a sporting event — I think it was a game at the local high school. The students then proceeded to create their own story problems based on the refreshments and souvenirs they might want to buy. I was never much interested in math as a child, but would have loved studying it with Nora. She let her students create the day's math lesson and, as a result, helped them put their learning in a meaningful context.

At the beginning I was convinced that the students would take more control of the project than they actually did. Part of negotiating the curriculum, however, involved accepting their need for direction and guiding them when they weren't inclined to make choices on their own.

Since my involvement in this project, I've found myself increasingly committed to providing a context for what my university students are learning, and to allowing them to negotiate their own curriculum. The students in my course on children's literature now have more voice in the texts they will read. Their final project involves selecting and evaluating several children's books on a topic of their choice. Perhaps more importantly, the assignment seems especially relevant because they are asked to choose these books for a specific school class, meeting the interests and age level of its children. Many of them tell me that they come to understand the value of what they are doing because of the context in which the assignment is given.

Skills in context

When I taught a course in writing for elementary teachers at Western Michigan University, I was sometimes disturbed by the writing assignments my students would propose. Invariably, some of them insisted on asking their students to write "a sentence" or "a paragraph." Most children, however, don't care a lot about writing sentences or paragraphs. Who makes a career out of writing sentences or paragraphs, anyway? I know I would much prefer to write a letter, a story, a newspaper article, a poem, a journal entry — in short, something authentic.

Many children don't care much about developing reading and writing skills out of context. Why should they care about the mechanics of writing a letter if they never plan to write one in their whole life? Why should a first-grader like my son care how to spell "hammer" and "ladder" (words on a recent spelling list he brought home) if he doesn't use them in his writing?

So one thing we conscientiously tried to do during the project was teach skills in context. After we had decided to write newspaper articles, for example, we then talked about the questions reporters ask. Since the children knew some of their work might appear in the weather anthology we were producing, spelling and mechanics became of greater interest. I found myself teaching mini-lessons on poetry, letter writing, ways to begin a short story — whatever the students needed as we tried different forms of writing.

Similarly, our discussion of meteorology grew out of books we read. The children's interests came first, then any skills or knowledge that would help them.

Once again I have found my experience with these first-graders useful in my university teaching, as when I recently taught a session on poetry as part of my class on literature for young adults, using Richard Peck's collection, *Sounds and Silences*. As usual I discovered that many of my students believed they didn't like poetry (despite the fact that they were mostly English majors), so, keeping what I'd learned from the children in mind, I decided to let the students select which poems we would read and discuss.

That particular day, virtually every student chose a poem about war, from a section on war which includes songs from the 60s such as "Where Have All the Flowers Gone?" Why? Because, as most of them indicated, those poems and songs were relevant — at that time the country was at war with Iraq. Poetry became meaningful to these adults when it dealt with their concerns and helped them articulate their feelings about world events.

Teacher roles in facilitating learning

One of my prime concerns during the project was to discover what it means to be a whole language teacher. Was I supposed to be a coach? A spectator? A catalyst?

Like Connie and Scott, Nora, Vickie and I came to believe that whole language teachers must be organizers who guide and direct student work, nurturing a community of teachers and learners. From the beginning Nora demonstrated many of the important qualities of a whole language teacher. In the following excerpts from my interview with Vickie, she discusses how Nora guided the children's learning and teaching, provided a good model for them and helped them to take risks.

Joel: How would you characterize Nora's teaching style?

Vickie: I have a lot of respect for Nora and think she's an excellent teacher. She has the knack of holding the class in the palm of her hand and getting them all involved so they're all excited. It doesn't make any difference if they're reading a book or doing mathematics or reading their papers. She can just get them excited. It's unusual for a teacher to be able to do that with a *whole* class.

Joel: How do you think she does this?

Vickie: By the questions she asks. The children will make a comment and she will say, "Well now, why did you say that?" Then they start to defend themselves to support what they said and the next thing you know they are all involved and every person has an opinion. The key is that they are not afraid to share their opinions. They're not afraid of criticism from anyone or from the teacher, because she's made it very clear that it's all right to make mistakes. It's all right if you're different — if you have an opinion different from someone else's. And she makes that very clear to her little first-graders.

The first time I entered her class, I noticed this. The children were not ho-hum. They were on the edge of their seats raising their hands, saying, "Hey, I want to participate in this conversation. This is my opinion."

She also helps them take risks by making them comfortable about sharing with the whole group. Any time a child writes a story or says something that is private or their own opinion, for a little person that's taking a risk. Every time you stand up in front of a group and say something that might be controversial, that's taking a risk.

That's why at 43 years old I'm afraid to get up in front of a group of people and talk, because that wasn't stressed when I was in school. You didn't take risks. I can remember the only time we got up and did anything orally in school was giving an oral book report. Maybe four times in my whole twelve years in school — the only times I ever shared. That's frightening. It's changing now.

Nora's kids started writing stories the very first day of class. They began sharing their stories, which is good. They get up in front of the class and aren't afraid to share. And if they choose not to share, that's fine, too.

Role-modeling

Nora, Vickie and I all demonstrated that we were readers and writers and students ourselves. We shared our enthusiasm about reading, our excitement about language, and our curiosity about the natural world. The children heard us reading aloud, saw us reading for ourselves. We took the time to enjoy tales of a town pelted with meatballs, of a boy who tries to save a snowball in his pocket, of a girl who tries to keep a lighthouse lit during a tremendous storm. When we read aloud, we sometimes made mistakes and corrected them. Sometimes we shared how we felt about a story. None of Nora's students could have left her class or our project without knowing that we three adults love to read and feel reading to be important.

Nora and Vickie also read aloud frequently outside of the project. At one point Vickie read to them from E.B. White's *Charlotte's Web*, after she had read them Beverly Cleary's *Ramona Quimby, Age Eight*.

We provided ample time for the children to read. It was clear how much we valued reading by the large chunks of time spent reading each day. Reading was never a punishment. It was a privilege and a joy. Vickie recounts one early experience that demonstrated the children's enthusiasm for reading: they got so excited about one story she was reading that the principal came in to discover the source of the commotion, and left pleasantly surprised to discover how excited the children were about a book.

We also shared our enthusiasm about writing. Nora and Vickie both wrote along with the children and shared what they wrote, orally and in the class book. In the course of discussing various kinds of writing, I tried to model how I might begin writing — what questions I might ask myself, what I would do first, how I might think over what I was doing.

We all had opportunities to show the children that teachers also make mistakes. In printing on the blackboard, I sometimes formed letters incorrectly, something the children were very quick to notice. Sometimes we would misspell a word, call a child by the wrong name, forget a page in a book we were reading. Nora, of course, was good at feigning a lack of knowledge about a number of things, getting the children to try to help her understand a particular concept.

Ultimately, we tried to help the children see that they, too, could read and write and that it was something they would want to do even as grown-ups.

Facilitating

During the project, Nora, Vickie and I became more than just role models. We soon found that we were also mentors and collaborators, facilitating the children's learning. We provided them with literary experiences by reading books aloud. We gave them vicarious experiences with weather through the *Reading Rainbow* episode, which showed them severe weather, and through experiments with making rainbows and flying paper airplanes. We also suggested topics and kinds of writing they might try. The following journal entry illustrates one moment when a teacher was needed to facilitate learning.

February 6

As part of today's session, we talked about how scientists have tried to make it rain. This was a logical outgrowth of our discussion of *Bringing the Rain to Kapiti Plain.* All well and good, I suppose. But the children didn't really understand what makes it rain in the first place. As a result, I found myself describing how raindrops develop and why they fall to the ground — in short, more direct teaching than I had planned.

At times, there seem to be so many little things we need to teach these first-graders so they can tackle larger issues or concepts. We *are* trying to teach them skills in context. In the end, it's important for us to help facilitate learning — providing the children with knowledge so they can actively participate in developing their own curriculum and make effective choices about it.

Like the teacher in de Jong's *The Wheel on the School,* we tried to stimulate the students to think for themselves, providing them with a knowledge base that they could then build upon. Indirect encouragement involved asking questions and brainstorming possibilities: What does "weather" mean? Why might some snow turn pink or green? What causes snow? How might we bring rain to Kapiti Plain? It also meant bringing the library to them, so that materials were accessible for their own explorations.

Sharing knowledge and experience

From my first day at Conway I found it nearly impossible *not* to share myself, my knowledge and my experience with Nora's students. First-graders have little compunction about asking personal questions and telling you exactly what they think. They vied for my attention, tried to give me gifts (drawings, pencils, paper hearts, paper airplanes), asked for my phone number, wanted to read about me. They wanted to know if I had children, where I lived, who my wife was. So it was natural that during the course of the project I shared some of what I claimed to know. Invariably this occurred in the context of class discussions. When we wrote about personal experiences, I shared my own mishaps with weather: my car stalling out on the freeway in the rain, a tornado warning in Kalamazoo. More importantly, however, I tried to share my own writing process — for instance, how I might go about writing a poem about rain, where I get my ideas, the mistakes I sometimes make.

Assisting learners in using what they know

The children in Nora's class actually knew a lot about weather already. They had all witnessed evaporation, knew that the wind was invisible, could identify rain clouds, had some concept of the seasons, had heard thunder. Since the subject matter of the project became their experience with weather, they were already experts. They had made snowmen, snow angels and snow forts. Like Peter of *The Snowy Day,* some of them had tried to save a snowball in their pocket. They had jumped in puddles and hidden in the cellar during a tornado warning.

Nevertheless, they weren't always aware of what they already knew. We had to help them discover and use their knowledge. Nora, Vickie and I all asked them questions. We brainstormed ideas and talked about our experiences, helping the students to become conscious of the knowledge they had already gained.

Collaborating

Much of the children's editing of their writing was put off until the end of the project. Earlier, most of the feedback they had received from of us and from each other had been positive, to encourage further writing. As a result, most of the children hadn't tried to polish what they had written.

Since these first-graders were just beginning to acquire writing skills, I literally became the editor of their work. In helping them revise, however, I tried to serve as partner. I was worried about appropriating their writing as my own, but also recognized that, when necessary, I needed to help them transform what they had written into something more intelligible. Since most of the children had no idea how to begin rewriting their work, I had them read their stories or poems aloud while I served as a translator of invented spellings and showed them how they might separate some of their words into sentences. Mostly, I tried to ask questions, taking down any changes the children wanted to make.

Although this exercise in revision seemed simply tacked on to everything else we had done, it was useful. The children got a taste of an important part of the writing process and their work remained their own. They had the ultimate say on any changes that were made. I also sought their input as to which pieces they most wanted to include in the class book. I enjoyed working with them one on one. They seemed to enjoy it, too, and many of them couldn't wait until it was their turn to come and sit with me.

Guiding discussion and research

Whole language teachers constantly guide students as they discuss and think about various topics. As in the fourth-grade project, this guidance frequently took the form of brainstorming. I have already mentioned many of the instances in which the class compiled word lists and discussed possible solutions to various problems. When we developed ideas about bringing the rain to Kapiti Plain and the causes of rainbows, the children benefited greatly from each other's ideas.

On other occasions, we were able to help guide them as they tackled new skills or tried new ideas. In a very literal way, Vickie guided them as they made paper airplanes and cloud pictures. Nora helped them construct their water cycle chart and create their big book on weather. At various times, Nora helped the children learn how to find information in the various science books in the classroom, and I talked about how to write newspaper articles and how to begin writing poems.

Relating new information to old

The best examples of drawing on prior knowledge and relating it to new information come from those moments when the class discussed specific aspects of the weather. In discussing the water cycle, Nora invited the children to consider what would happen to a glass of water if they left it outside. They already knew the answer. Then she helped them relate the concept of evaporation to the water cycle as a whole. Vickie used their prior knowledge of what clouds look like to discuss types of clouds. In writing stories and poems, we took what the children already knew about titles and the beginnings of books to help them see how to construct their own works.

What was interesting to me was how much knowledge the children actually brought with them about the many topics we discussed. Many of them, for example, already understood quite well what causes a rainstorm.

Assessment and evaluation

When I first went to Conway, evaluation was the farthest thing from my mind. There was no place in the students' report cards to evaluate the kind of work I hoped they would do. Moreover, I would not have the opportunity to work enough with individual students to chart their progress in reading or writing.

In any case, as for Connie and Scott in the fourth-grade project, we were reluctant to evaluate the students, particularly since we weren't sure where the project was taking us and since we felt that a great concern with evaluation might dampen the students' interest in what we were going to do. Nevertheless, although we weren't always conscious we were doing it, we evaluated both the students and ourselves throughout the project.

Ken Goodman, in his preface to *The Whole Language Evaluation Book,* suggests that whole language teachers use student behaviors "as indications of developing knowledge and underlying competence." He goes on to talk about informal evaluation, suggesting that there "is always a learning function as well as an evaluative function: readers may discuss their own miscues; peer-editing conferences may offer constructive criticism; a test stemming from unit-based concepts may refocus discussion and stimulate reflective thinking; a group project may distill knowledge gained from reading and discussion." (p.xiii) Perhaps most importantly, he maintains that most whole language teachers generally use interaction, observation and analysis when they evaluate.

Teacher evaluation of students

The students in Nora's class were constantly being evaluated in the sense that they responded to each other's work, reacted to questions we asked them, and edited what they wrote for publication in the class book. Our interactions with them, our observation of their responses to the project, and our analysis of their work helped to shape the project itself. They in turn evaluated the project on a daily basis — they were very open about what they liked and did not like. They weren't much interested in informational books, for example. It was hard to keep their attention when I read them a book about weather forecasting. On the other hand, they loved stories and wanted to read and write them. Their openness certainly shaped everything that happened.

Student self-evaluation

Towards the end of the project, I tried to get Nora's class to articulate how they felt about the project and to assess their part in it. They were not as introspective as Connie and Scott's fourth-graders, but they honestly admitted, for example, that they didn't always cooperate with one another.

Nevertheless, they were proud of the work they had done. They thought of themselves as writers and took pleasure in the stories they had written and the books they had read. Even the shyest students eventually shared what they had written with the group. Often, they finished a piece of writing and looked for another idea to begin writing something else. This was not, of course, the result of the project itself. They had worked together since the beginning of the year, reading and sharing books and sharing their writing with each other. Their self-confidence had constantly been fostered by Nora, at least in part because she practiced most of the whole language principles we've discussed. What the project may have contributed was helping them focus their energy and experiment with different forms of reading and writing.

Student evaluation of the project

Like Connie and Scott, I asked the students to evaluate the project. I started out by asking them to write me a letter telling me what they liked about it. Since I didn't want to influence what they wrote, however, I didn't encourage prior discussion. As a result, their letters centered almost exclusively on the factual information they had gained and on which activities were fun. Some ignored my directions altogether and wrote more new stories about their experiences with the weather.

The following are some of their responses, edited for spelling and punctuation:

I have learned some things. I have learned that tornados have been in some cities and one tornado came through Donovan. I like you.

I like studying air. Air is fun to study.

I liked the rain and the tornado and the clouds and the wind and the water cycle and the air and the snow and the hail. The end.

I learned a lot since you have been here. I will share some things I learned. You can't fly an airplane unless there is air. I like that time that we flew airplanes. Thank you for everything.

> I've learned about weather.
> One thing I liked was the
> water cycle because it was fun.

> I liked learning
> about tornados.

> I like how you taught
> us to make a rainbow.

In hopes of getting more specific evaluation, I talked about the project with the students during our editing conferences. Even then they had a hard time getting beyond describing which activities they liked, though they now offered a wider variety of responses. From what they told me, it became clear that most of the class liked the following aspects of the project:

~ reading stories aloud as a class
~ writing stories about themselves
~ class activities (flying paper airplanes and creating cloud pictures)
~ illustrating what they had written
~ reading individually stories that had been read aloud
~ learning why certain types of weather develop
~ discussing certain types of weather, particularly tornados and thunderstorms

Eventually I was able to develop another list by approaching their evaluation from another angle. I began asking them to articulate what they liked and didn't like about the reading and writing we did together. Here is the second list of their likes:

~ choosing their own writing assignments
~ sharing what they'd written
~ publishing their work
~ choosing their own books
~ reading to others in the class
~ talking about things before they wrote them
~ drawing pictures as part of their writing
~ personal attention from the teachers
~ the teacher's help when they were trying new kinds of writing

Of course, a few dislikes also appeared. Some of the children didn't like writing every day. Some also lost interest in the topic of weather during the last couple of weeks. Most of this was not surprising — I was also a little tired of weather towards the end!

In any case, their "likes" supported many of the whole language principles we've discussed. The children certainly liked some degree of independence and appreciated the fact that their opinions and ideas were valued.

Final reflections on our goals

As I've already mentioned, at the start of the project I was very concerned with the practical aspects of whole language teaching and whether or not it was really possible with first-graders. I discovered, of course, that whole language is both practical and possible. It was clear that these first-graders responded well to the way we approached the theme.

Along the way, I also realized that whole language is more than just a list of rules. Unlike Arnold Lobel's Toad, who became a slave to his list of things to do, we couldn't let ourselves be ruled by our initial understanding of the principles we espoused.

I do have some regrets, however. Our project might have been more integrative, drawing more heavily on other aspects of the curriculum. I might have used peer editing more effectively. The class could have experimented more with science.

But these things relate to the project as a product. When viewing it as a process, I am pleased with my own growth. I let the students take more control than is usual when I teach and learned a lot from Nora and Vickie about what whole language teachers are and can become. No longer do I believe that becoming a whole language teacher is impossible. It takes work and energy, but is definitely worth it.

Final reflections on the project

Again like Connie and Scott, I feel that during the regular school year a unit like the one we did on weather would need to be balanced with topics that emphasize something other than science. With students in the early elementary grades, these theme explorations might well need to be shorter than the one we attempted, if only to help keep the students interested.

And they should always be collaborations between teacher and students, so that both students and teacher will make the kind of discoveries described in *A Ring of Endless Light,* discoveries that come from "two completely different imaginations working together and being far more than either one alone." (p.241)

The voyage continues

~ ~ ~ ~ ~

In the introduction we warned our readers that this would be an intensely personal book. In describing our "voyage of discovery" we have confessed our doubts and shortcomings, cataloged our "mistakes" and celebrated our successes. We've shared some of the important discoveries we made about ourselves as teachers, about whole language, theme exploration and the needs and capabilities of first- and fourth-graders. We've lamented that we didn't always make the most of the opportunities that arose for teaching and learning, and that we were forced to abandon some of the activities we planned as part of our theme exploration project — or at least as part of our initial vision of it.

Connie would have liked to continue the literature discussions on *Cracker Jackson*. Joel longed for some real weather experiments. Scott wanted the students in the environment group to initiate or become involved in some environment preservation project outside of school. We learned, however, that if teachers want students to help negotiate the curriculum, they must sometimes subordinate their own ideas and interests to those of their students. And we were reminded that lack of time is always an obstacle to accomplishing what we initially envision.

At the same time, we feel that both parts of our project were successful.

~ We achieved many of our goals (see chapters five and six).

~ The students not only learned facts, but also developed interests and attitudes and values that would have been left untouched by a more traditional thematic unit.

~ In general, we gave the students control of their own learning, without foisting our "good ideas" onto them.

~ We confirmed for ourselves that whole language is not only possible, but also practical in schools with a fairly structured curriculum.

~ We reaffirmed our belief that first-graders as well as fourth-graders can read and write and think for themselves when given opportunity and encouragement.

~ We proved that theme explorations are possible without canned, mechanical teaching units like those we would expect from the spelling teacher on Camazotz in L'Engle's *A Wrinkle in Time*.

Perhaps most important for leaving us with the feeling of success are the discoveries we made, especially about negotiating the curriculum:

~ We learned that students can be and enjoy being responsible for helping to shape the classroom curriculum.

~ We learned that curriculum needs to be constantly renegotiated. It won't do to make decisions and never reevaluate them.

~ We learned that negotiating the curriculum involves a continuous ebb and flow. Sometimes the teacher offers new ideas and the students respond; sometimes the students suggest changes and the teacher responds to their interests and needs.

~ We learned that negotiating the curriculum does not preclude planning or teaching. Teachers are necessary to facilitate learning.

We were continually faced with new challenges that stimulated discoveries and reaffirmed established beliefs. It was exciting to acquire an ever-deeper understanding of some of the principles that characterize a whole language philosophy, to put into practice more and more of what we understood about that philosophy and to gain in turn, from reflecting on our experiences, an even richer understanding.

Collaborating on this book, too, has been an experience in whole language. In negotiating the content and structure, we all had to relinquish control. We all took risks. On the other hand, we've all had the chance to become role models, students, facilitators, editors and cheerleaders, encouraging one another in our individual voyages of discovery.

We are still growing into whole language. We know our voyage isn't over, that we are still reaching toward the "infinitely receding shore" Connie described in the introduction. All of us will continue to teach, research and grow, exploring other aspects of whole language that interest us: the role of literature in whole language classrooms, oral and written language and literature as vehicles for learning in science and social studies, portfolio assessment, to name a few. We are still in the process of becoming "real" whole language teachers, attempting to practice the principles we've espoused in both college and public school classrooms.

Like the teacher in *The Wheel on the School,* we hope that we can grow in our ability to facilitate our students' learning, and that by offering them meaningful learning experiences we can help them to continue their own voyages of discovery.

~ ~ ~ ~ ~ ~
# Bibliographies
~ ~ ~ ~

Children's books

The following books have been cited in the text of this book, as have the marked titles in Appendix 3, which contains a sample bibliography of theme-related children's titles (pages 224-230).

Fiction

Asimov, Isaac, Patricia Warren and Martin Greenberg, eds. 1983. *Machines That Think: The Best Science Fiction Stories about Robots and Computers*. New York: Henry Holt.

Asimov, Janet and Isaac. 1983. *The Norby Chronicles*. New York: Berkley.

Atwater, Richard and Florence. 1938. *Mr. Popper's Penguins*. Illus. Robert Lawson. Boston: Little, Brown.

Barrett, Judi. 1978. *Cloudy With a Chance of Meatballs*. Illus. Ron Barrett. New York: Atheneum.

Bauer, Caroline Feller, ed. 1986. *Snowy Day: Stories and Poems*. Illus. Margot Tomes. New York: Lippincott.

Bradbury, Ray. 1969. *I Sing the Body Electric!* New York: Alfred A. Knopf.

Byars, Betsy. 1985. *Cracker Jackson*. New York: Viking.

Cleary, Beverly. 1982. *Ramona Quimby, Age Eight*. Dell.

Cooney, Barbara. 1982. *Miss Rumphius*. New York: Penguin.

Crowe, Robert L. 1980. *Tyler Toad and the Thunder*. Illus. Kay Chorao. New York: Dutton.

de Angeli, Marguerite. 1949. *The Door in the Wall*. New York: Doubleday. [Also Scholastic]

DeJong, Meindert. 1954. *The Wheel on the School*. New York: Harper & Row.

de Treviño, Elizabeth Borton. 1965. *I, Juan de Pareja*. New York: Farrar, Strauss & Giroux.

George, Jean Craighead. 1975. *My Side of the Mountain*. New York: Dutton. [Also Scholastic]

Hillert, Margaret. 1969. *The Snow Baby*. Illus. Liz Dauber. Chicago: Follett.

Hunter, Mollie. 1975. *A Stranger Came Ashore*. New York: Harper & Row.

Keats, Ezra Jack. 1962. *The Snowy Day*. New York: Viking. [Also Scholastic]

Lee, Harper. 1960. *To Kill a Mockingbird*. New York: Lippincott.

L'Engle, Madeleine. 1962. *A Wrinkle in Time*. New York: Farrar, Straus & Giroux.

———. 1980. *A Ring of Endless Light*. New York: Farrar, Straus & Giroux.

Lester, Helen. 1988. *Tacky the Penguin*. Boston: Houghton Mifflin.

Lobel, Arnold. 1971. *Frog and Toad Together*. New York: Harper & Row. [Also Scholastic]

McCloskey, Robert. 1957. *Time of Wonder*. New York: Macmillan.

McKissack, Patricia. 1988. *Mirandy and Brother Wind*. New York: Alfred A. Knopf.

Marney, Dean. 1985. *The Computer That Ate My Brother*. New York: Scholastic.

Nostlinger, Christine. 1977. *Konrad*. Trans. Anthea Bell. New York: Watts.

Palin, Michael, Alan Lee and Richard Seymor. 1986. *The Mirrorstone*. Alfred A. Knopf.

Paterson, Katherine. 1977. *Bridge to Terabithia*. New York: Harper & Row.

Paulsen, Gary. 1988. *The Island*. New York: Dell.

Rawls, Wilson. 1977. *Summer of the Monkeys*. New York: Dell.

Robinson, Barbara. 1972. *The Best Christmas Pageant Ever*. New York: Harper & Row.

Rock, Gail. 1975. *The House Without a Christmas Tree*. New York: Alfred A. Knopf. [Also Scholastic]

Roop, Peter and Connie. 1985. *Keep the Lights Burning, Abbie*. Minneapolis: Carolrhoda. [Also Scholastic]

Speare, Elizabeth George. 1961. *The Bronze Bow*. New York: Houghton Mifflin.

——. 1958. *The Witch of Blackbird Pond*. New York: Houghton Mifflin.

Spier, Peter. 1982. *Rain*. New York: Doubleday.

Stolz, Mary. 1988. *Storm in the Night*. Illus. Pat Cummings. New York: Harper & Row.

Twain, Mark. 1983. *The Adventures of Tom Sawyer*. New York: Penguin. [Also Scholastic]

Walker, Alice. 1976. *The Color Purple*. New York: Simon & Schuster.

White, E. B. 1952. *Charlotte's Web*. New York: Harper & Row. [Also Scholastic]

——. 1945. *Stuart Little*. New York: Harper & Row. [Also Scholastic]

Zolotow, Charlotte. 1952. *The Storm Book*. New York: Harper & Row.

Nonfiction

Abrams, Malcolm and Harriet Bernstein. 1989. *Future Stuff*. New York: Penguin.

Adler, David. 1983. *World of Weather*. Illus. Ray Burns. Mahuah, NJ: Troll.

Bellamy, David. 1988. *The River*. Illus. Jill Dow. New York: Clarkson N. Potter. Distributed by Crown. [Also Scholastic]

Brandt, Keith. 1982. *What Makes It Rain: The Story of a Raindrop*. Mahuah, NJ: Troll.

Branley, Franklin M. 1985. *Flash, Crash, Rumble, and Roll*. Illus. Barbara and Ed Emberley. Rev. ed. New York: Harper & Row.

——. 1985. *Hurricane Watch*. Illus. Giulio Maestro. New York: Harper & Row.

——. 1986. *Air Is All Around You*. Illus. Holly Keller. Rev. ed. New York: Harper & Row.

——. 1986. *Snow Is Falling*. Illus. Holly Keller. Rev. ed. New York: Harper & Row.

——. 1987. *It's Raining Cats and Dogs: All Kinds of Weather and Why We Have It*. Boston: Houghton Mifflin.

——. 1988. *Tornado Alert*. Illus. Giulio Maestro. New York: Harper & Row.

de Paola, Tomie. 1975. *The Cloud Book*. New York: Holiday House. [Also Scholastic]

Earth Works Group. 1990. *50 Simple Things You Can Do to Save the Earth*. Schenevus, NY: Greenleaf.

Javna, John. 1990. *50 Simple Things Kids Can Do to Save the Earth*. Kansas City, MO: Andrews & McMeel. [Also Scholastic]

Lauber, Patricia. 1987. *Get Ready for Robots*. New York: Harper & Row.

Liptak, Karen. 1984. *Robotics Basics*. Illus. Mike Petronella. Englewood Cliffs, NJ: Prentice-Hall.

Martin, Claire. 1987. *I Can Be a Weather Forecaster*. Chicago: Children's Press.

Milton, Joyce. 1981. *Here Come the Robots*. Illus. Peter Stern. New York: Hastings House; Don Mills, ON: Saunders.

Rourke Enterprises. 1983. *Animal World: The Penguin*. Mahwah, NJ: Watermill Press.

Simon, Seymour. 1989. *Storms*. New York: William Morrow. [Also Scholastic]

Terkel, Studs. 1985. *Working*. New York: Ballantine.

Wyatt, Valerie. 1990. *Weather Watch*. Illus. Pat Cupples. Toronto: Kids Can Press.

Poetry

Aardema, Verna. 1981. *Bringing the Rain to Kapiti Plain*. Illus. Beatriz Vidal. New York: Dial. [Also Scholastic]

Bauer, Caroline, ed. 1986. *Snowy Day: Stories and Poems*. Illus. Margot Tomes. New York: Lippincott.

Peck, Richard, ed. 1970. *Sounds and Silences: Poetry for Now*. New York: Doubleday.

Prelutsky, Jack, ed. 1983. *The Random House Book of Poetry for Children*. New York: Random House.

Aids for selecting children's books

The following published books, bibliographies, and review sources will provide assistance in selecting theme-related books. Other titles that include bibliographies useful for book selection have been marked in the "Professional books and articles" section.

Bibliographies

Benedict, Susan. 1991. *Beyond Words: Picture Books for Older Readers and Writers*. Portsmouth, NH: Heinemann.

Booth, David, Larry Swartz and Meguido Zola. 1987.*Choosing Children's Books*. Markham, ON: Pembroke.

Bosma, Bette. 1992. *Fairy Tales, Fables, Legends, and Myths: Using Folk Literature in Your Classroom*. New York: Teachers College Press.

Davis, James E. and Hazel K. Davis, eds. 1988. *Your Reading: A Booklist for Junior High and Middle School Students*. Urbana, IL: National Council of Teachers of English.

Dreyer, Sharon. 1977. *The Bookfinder: A Guide to Children's Literature About the Needs and Problems of Youth Aged 2-15*. Circle Pines, MN: American Guidance Service.

Freeman, Judy. 1990. *Books Kids Will Sit Still For*. 2nd ed. New York: Bowker.

Gagnon, André and Ann Gagnon, eds. 1988. *Canadian Books for Young People/Livres canadiens pour la jeunesse*. 4th ed. Toronto: University of Toronto Press.

Gillespie, John and Christine B. Gilbert. 1990. *Best Books for Children: Preschool Through the Middle Grades*. 4th ed. New York: Bowker.

Jett-Simpson, Mary, ed. 1989. *Adventuring with Books: A Booklist for Pre-K–Grade 6*. 9th ed. Urbana, IL: National Council of Teachers of English.

Kennedy, Day Ann M., Stella S. Spangler and Mary Ann Vanderwerf. 1990. *Science and Technology in Fact and Fiction: A Guide to Children's Books*. New York: Bowker.

Kobrin, Beverly. 1988. *Eyeopeners!: How to Choose and Use Children's Books about Real People, Places, and Things*. New York: Viking Penguin.

Landsberg, Michele. 1986. *Michele Landsberg's Guide to Children's Books*. Toronto, ON: Penguin.

Lima, Carolyn W. and John A. Lima, eds. 1989. *A to Zoo: Subject Access to Children's Picture Books*. 3rd ed. New York: Bowker.

Moir, Hughes, Melissa Cain and Leslie Prosak-Beres, eds. 1990. *Collected Perspectives: Choosing and Using Books for the Classroom*. Norwood, MA.: Christopher-Gordon.

Nilson, Alleen Pace, ed. 1991. *Your Reading: A Booklist for Junior High and Middle School Students*. 8th ed. Urbana, IL: National Council of Teachers of English

Nilson, Lenore, comp. 1988. *The Best of Children's Choices*. Ed. Jane Charlton. Ottawa, ON: Citizens' Committee on Children.

Norton, Donna. 1991. *Through the Eyes of a Child: An Introduction to Children's Literature*. 3rd ed. New York: Macmillan.

Oppenheim, Joanne, Barbara Brenner and Betty D. Boegehold. 1986. *Choosing Books for Kids: How to Choose the Right Book for the Right Child at the Right Time*. New York: Ballantine.

Peterson, Barbara. 1991. "Selecting Books for Beginning Readers." *Bridges to Literacy: Learning from Reading Recovery*. Diane E. DeFord, Carol A. Lyons and Gay Su Pinnell, eds. Portsmouth, NH: Heinemann.

Sinclair, Patti. 1992. *E for Environment: An Annotated Bibliography of Children's Books with Environmental Themes*. New York: Bowker.

Subject Guide to Children's Books in Print. New York: Bowker. [Annual]

Sutherland, Zena. 1986. *The Best in Children's Picture Books: The University of Chicago Guide to Children's Literature, 1979-1984*. Chicago: University of Chicago Press.

Sutherland, Zena and May Hill Arbuthnot. 1991. *Children and Books*. 8th ed. New York: HarperCollins.

Trelease, Jim. 1985. *The Read-Aloud Handbook*. Revised edition. New York: Viking.

——. 1989. *The New Read-Aloud Handbook*. New York: Penguin.

VanMeter, Vandelia. 1990. *American History for Children and Young Adults: An Annotated Index*. Englewood, CO: Libraries Unlimited.

Wilms, Denise M., ed. *Science Books for Children: Selections from Booklist, 1976-1983*. Chicago: American Library Association.

Winkel, Lois. 1988. *The Elementary School Library Collection: A Guide to Books and Other Media*. 16th ed. Bro-Dart.

Wittig, Alice J. 1989. *U.S. Government Publications for the School Media Center*. Englewood, CO: Libraries Unlimited.

Periodicals with reviews

Book Links. Chicago, IL: American Library Assosiation.

Booklist, ed. Bill Ott. Chicago, IL: American Library Assosiation.

CCL: Canadian Children's Literature/Littérature canadienne pour la jeunesse. Guelph, ON: Canadian Children's Press/Canadian Children's Literature Association, University of Guelph.

CM: Canadian Materials. Ottawa, ON: Canadian Library Association.

The Children's Book News. Toronto, ON: Canadian Children's Book Centre.

Children's Literature in Education. New York: Human Sciences Press (Subsidiary of Plenum).

The Horn Book Magazine. Boston: Horn Book Inc.

Language Arts. Urbana, IL: National Council of Teachers of English.

The Lion and the Unicorn. Baltimore, MD: Johns Hopkins University Press.

The Reading Teacher. Newark, DE: International Reading Association.

Science and Children. [Bibliography in the March issue] Washington, DC: National Science Teacher Association.

School Library Journal. New York: Cahners Publishing (Subsidiary of Reed Publishing)

Teachers Networking. Katonah, NY: Richard C. Owen.

Professional books and articles

These professional materials provide useful background information for theme exploration in whole language classrooms. For convenient reference, they have been coded as follows:

* These titles have been cited in the text of the book.

+ These books help to define and characterize whole language.

‡ These books describe language and literacy acquisition.

† These books describe whole language assessment.

¤ These books describe whole language practices in the classroom.

^ These books describe theme study (not necessarily whole language).

° These books include extensive annotated bibliographies.

+ Altwerger, Bess. 1991. "Whole Language Teachers: Empowered Professionals." *Whole Language: Empowerment at the Chalkface*, 15-29. J. Hydrick, ed. New York: Scholastic.

+ Altwerger, Bess, Carole Edelsky and Barbara M. Flores. November, 1987. "Whole Language: What's new?" *The Reading Teacher* 41: 144-154.

^ ¤ Altwerger, Bess and E. Saavedra. February, 1989. "Thematic Units vs. Theme Cycles." Workshop presented at CEL conference, Winnipeg.

† Anthony, Robert, Terry D. Johnson, Jim Field, Norma Mickelson and Alison Preece. 1991. *Evaluating Literacy: A Perspective for Change*. Portsmouth, NH: Heinemann.

° ¤ * Atwell, Nancie. 1987. *In the Middle: Writing, Reading, and Learning with Adolescents*. Portsmouth, NH: Heinemann.

¤ ——, ed. 1990. *Coming to Know: Writing to Learn in the Intermediate Grades*. Portsmouth, NH: Heinemann.

‡ Baghban, M. 1984. *Our Daughter Learns to Read and Write: A Case Study from Birth to Three*. Newark, DE: International Reading Association.

† Barrs, Myra, Sue Ellis, Hilary Tester and Anne Thomas [Centre for Language in Primary Education]. 1989. *The Primary Language Record: Handbook for Teachers*. Portsmouth, NH: Heinemann.

† Baskwill, Jane and Paulette Whitman. 1988. *Evaluation: Whole Language, Whole Child*. Richmond Hill, ON: Scholastic.

¤ ——. 1986. *Whole Language Sourcebook, Grades K-2*. Richmond Hill, ON: Scholastic.

¤ ——. 1988. *Whole Language Sourcebook, Grades 3-4*. Richmond Hill, ON: Scholastic.

¤ Baskwill, Jane and Steve. 1991. *Whole Language Sourcebook, Grades 5-6*. Richmond Hill, ON: Scholastic.

† Belanoff, Pat and Marcia Dickson. 1991. *Portfolio Grading: Process and Product*. Portsmouth, NH: Boynton-Cook.

‡ Bissex, G. 1980. *GNYS AT WRK: A Child Learns to Write and Read*. Cambridge, MA: Harvard University Press.

¤ *Bookshelf, Stage 1 Resource Book*. 1986. New York: Scholastic.

‡ Brown, Roger. 1973. *A First Language: The Early Stages*. Cambridge: Harvard University Press.

¤ Butler, Andrea. 1984. *The Story Box in the Classroom, Stage 1*. Bothell, WA: Rigby Education; distributed by The Wright Group.

California State Department of Education. 1987. *English-Language Arts Framework*. Sacramento, CA: California State Department of Education.

¤ Calkins, Lucy McCormick. May, 1980. "When children want to punctuate: Basic skills belong in context." *Language Arts* 57: 567-573. Also in *Children Want to Write . . . Donald Graves in Australia*, 89-96 R.D. Walshe, ed. Portsmouth, NH: Heinemann.

¤ ——. 1983. *Lessons from a Child*. Portsmouth, NH: Heinemann.

¤ * ——. 1986. *The Art of Teaching Writing*. Portsmouth, NH: Heinemann.

¤ ——. 1990. *Living Between the Lines*. Portsmouth, NH: Heinemann.

¤ + Cambourne, Brian. 1988. *The Whole Story: Natural Learning and the Acquisition of Literacy in the Classsroom*. Auckland, New Zealand: Ashton Scholastic.

¤ + Center for the Expansion of Dialogue. 1990. *Literature Study: Karen Smith's Classroom*. Videotape. Tucson, AZ: CED.

‡ Clay, Marie. 1975. *What Did I Write?* Portsmouth, NH: Heinemann.

‡ ——. 1987. *Writing Begins at Home*. Portsmouth, NH: Heinemann.

‡ ——. 1991. *Becoming Literate: The Construction of Inner Control*. Portsmouth, NH: Heinemann.

Cottrell, June. 1987. *Creative Drama in the Classroom: Grades 1-3*. Lincolnwood, IL: National Textbook Company.

———. 1987. *Creative Drama in the Classroom: Grades 4-6*. Lincolnwood, IL: National Textbook Company.

¤ † Daly, Elizabeth, ed. 1990. *Monitoring Children's Language Development: Holistic Assessment in Classrooms*. Portsmouth, NH: Heinemann.

¤ † De Fina, Allan A. 1992. *Portfolio Assessment: Getting Started*. New York: Scholastic.

‡ Doake, David. 1988. *Reading Begins at Birth*. Richmond Hill, ON: Scholastic.

Durkin, Dolores. May, 1990. "Are the New Basals Any Better?" Paper presented at the International Reading Association convention, Atlanta.

^ + Edelsky, Carole, Bess Altwerger and Barbara Flores. 1991. *Whole Language: What's the Difference?* Portsmouth, NH: Heinemann.

+ Edelsky, Carole and Karen Draper. 1989. "Reading/'reading'; writing/'writing'; text/'text.'" *Reading-Canada-Lecture* 7: 201-216.

+ Edelsky, Carole and Karen Smith. January, 1984. "Is that writing — or are those marks just a figment of your curriculum?" *Language Arts* 61: 24-32.

¤ * Eeds, Maryann and Deborah Wells. February, 1989. "Grand conversations: An exploration of meaning construction in literature study groups." *Research in the Teaching of English* 23: 4-29.

¤ † Eggleton, J. 1990. *Whole Language Evaluation: Reading, Writing, and Spelling*. Bothell, WA: The Wright Group.

Emig, Janet. 1983. "Non-magical thinking: Presenting writing developmentally in schools." *The Web of Meaning: Essays on Writing, Teaching, Learning, and Thinking*, 133-44. Portsmouth, NH: Boynton/Cook.

‡ + Ferreiro, E. and A. Teberosky. 1982. *Literacy Before Schooling*. K.G. Castro, trans. Portsmouth, NH: Heinemann.

‡ + Fields, Marjorie V. May, 1988. "Talking and writing: Explaining the whole language approach to parents." *The Reading Teacher* 41: 898-903.

¤ † Fisher, B. 1991. *Joyful Learning: A Whole Language Kindergarten*. Portsmouth, NH: Heinemann.

+ Freeman, Yvonne S. Summer, 1989. "Literature-based or literature: Where do we stand?" *Teachers Networking* 9: 13-15.

^ Gamberg, Ruth, Winnifred Kwak, Meredith Hutchings, Judy Altheim, with Gail Edwards. 1988. *Learning and Loving It: Theme*

Studies in the Classroom. Portsmouth, NH: Heinemann; Toronto: OISE Press.

Giacobbe, Mary Ellen. 1984. "Helping children become more responsible for their own writing." *LiveWire* 1(i): 7-9. Urbana, IL: National Council of Teachers of English.

¤ Glover, Mary Kenner. 1992. *Charlie's Ticket to Literacy*. Richmond Hill, ON: Scholastic.

Goodman, Kenneth. October, 1965. "A linguistic study of cues and miscues in reading." *Elementary English* 42: 639-643.

———. 1982. *Language and Literacy: The Selected Writings of Kenneth S. Goodman*. Frederick V. Gollasch, ed. 2 vols. Boston: Routledge and Kegan Paul.

+ ———. 1986. *What's Whole in Whole Language?* Richmond Hill, ON: Scholastic. [Also Heinemann in USA]

+ ———. November, 1989. "Whole-language research: Foundations and development." *The Elementary School Journal* 90: 208-221.

+ Goodman, Kenneth S., Lois Bird Bridges and Yetta M. Goodman. 1990. *The Whole Language Catalog*. Santa Rosa, CA: American School Publishers.

¤ † ———. 1992. *Authentic Assessment: Supplement to The Whole Language Catalog*. Santa Rosa, CA: American School Publishers.

‡ Goodman, Kenneth S. and Yetta M. Goodman. 1979. "Learning to read is natural." *Theory and Practice of Early Reading*. Lauren B. Resnick and Phyllis A Weaver, eds. 1: 137-154. Hillsdale, NJ: Erlbaum.

† * Goodman, Kenneth S., Yetta M. Goodman and Wendy J. Hood. 1989. *The Whole Language Evaluation Book*. Portsmouth, NH: Heinemann.

Goodman, Kenneth S., Patrick Shannon, Yvonne Freeman and Sharon Murphy. 1988. *Report Card on Basal Readers*. Katonah, NY: Richard C. Owen.

† + Goodman, Yetta M. June, 1978. "Kid watching: An alternative to testing." *National Elementary School Principal* 57: 41-45.

+ ———. November, 1989. "Roots of the whole-language movement." *The Elementary School Journal* 90: 113-127.

‡ ———, ed. 1990. *How Children Construct Literacy: Piagetian Perspectives*. Newark, DE: International Reading Association.

¤ † ———. 1992. "Bookhandling Knowledge Task." *Authentic Assessment: Supplement to the Whole Language Catalog*, 140. Kenneth S.

Goodman, Lois Bird Bridges and Yetta M. Goodman, eds. Santa Rosa, CA: American School Publishers.

¤ † Goodman, Yetta M. and Bess Altwerger. 1986. "Pre-schoolers' book handling knowledge." Included in *Bookshelf, Stage 1 Resource Book*. New York: Scholastic.

Goodman, Yetta and Carolyn L. Burke. 1980. *Reading Strategies: Focus on Comprehension*. Katonah, NY: Richard C. Owen.

† Goodman, Yetta, Dorothy J. Watson and Carolyn L. Burke. 1987. *Reading Miscue Inventory: Alternative Procedures*. Katonah, NY: Richard C. Owen.

Goswami, Dixie and Peter R. Stillman, eds. 1987. *Reclaiming the Classroom Teacher: Research as an Agency for Change*. Portsmouth, NH: Heinemann.

Graves, Donald. September, 1976. "Let's get rid of the welfare mess in the teaching of writing." *Language Arts* 53: 645-651.

¤ ——. 1983. *Writing: Teachers and Children at Work*. Portsmouth, NH: Heinemann.

——. 1989. *Experiment with Fiction*. Portsmouth, NH: Heinemann.

——. 1989. *Investigate Nonfiction*. Portsmouth, NH: Heinemann.

¤ † Graves, D.H. and B.S. Sundstein, eds. 1992. *Portfolio Portraits*. Portsmouth, NH: Heinemann.

+ Gursky, D. August, 1991. "After the Reign of Dick and Jane." *Teacher Magazine*, 22-29.

¤ + Hall, Nigel. 1987. *The Emergence of Literacy*. Portsmouth, NH: Heinemann.

‡ Halliday, M.A.K. 1975. *Learning How to Mean: Explorations in the Development of Language*. London: Edward Arnold.

¤ Hancock, Joelie and Susan Hill, eds. 1987. *Literature-Based Reading Programs at Work*. Portsmouth, NH: Heinemann.

¤ * Hansen, Jane. 1987. *When Writers Read*. Portsmouth, NH: Heinemann.

¤ Hansen, Jane, Tom Newkirk and Donald M. Graves, eds. 1985. *Breaking Ground: Teachers Relate Reading and Writing in the Elementary School*. Portsmouth, NH: Heinemann.

¤ † Harp, Bill, ed. 1991. *Assessment and Evaluation in Whole Language Programs*. Norwood, MA: Christopher-Gordon.

+ Harste, Jerome C. 1989. *New Policy Guidelines for Reading: Connecting Research and Practice*. Urbana, IL: National Council of Teachers of English.

° ¤ Harste, Jerome C., Kathy G. Short, with Carolyn L. Burke. 1988. *Creating Classrooms for Authors: The Reading-Writing Connection.* Portsmouth, NH: Heinemann.

‡ Harste, Jerome C., Virginia A. Woodward and Carolyn L. Burke. 1984. *Language Stories and Literacy Lessons.* Portsmouth, NH: Heinemann.

* Hartwell, Patrick. February, 1985. "Grammar, grammars, and the teaching of grammar." *College English* 47: 105-127.

* Heimlich, Joan E. and Susan D. Pittelman. 1986. *Semantic Mapping: Classroom Applications.* Newark, DE: International Reading Association.

Heinig, Ruth. 1987. *Creative Drama Resource Book for Grades 4 through 6.* Englewood Cliffs, NJ: Prentice-Hall.

———. 1987. *Creative Drama Resource Book for Kindergarten through Grade 3.* Englewood Cliffs, NJ: Prentice-Hall.

‡ Hill, Mary W. 1989. *Home: Where Reading and Writing Begin.* Portsmouth, NH: Heinemann.

Holdaway, Don. 1979. *The Foundations of Literacy.* Sydney, Australia: Ashton Scholastic. [Heinemann in USA]

+ ———. 1986. "The structure of natural learning as a basis for literacy instruction." *The Pursuit of Literacy: Early Reading and Writing,* 56-72. Michael R. Sampson, ed. Dubuque, IA: Kendall Hunt.

^ Jobe, Ron and Paula Hart. 1991. *Canadian Connections: Experiencing Literature with Children.* Markham, ON: Pembroke.

¤ † Johnson, Terry D., Robert Anthony, Jim Field, Norma Mickelson and Alison Preece. 1988. *Evaluation: A Perspective for Change.* Crystal Lake, IL: Rigby.

¤ Johnson, Terry D. and Daphne R. Louis. 1987. *Literacy Through Literature.* Richmond Hill, ON: Scholastic. [Heinemann in USA]

¤ ———. 1990. *Bringing It All Together: A Program for Literacy.* Richmond Hill, ON: Scholastic. [Heinemann in USA]

Kelly, E., Carl Rogers, Abraham Maslow and A. Combs. 1962. *Perceiving, Behaving, Becoming.* New York: Association for Supervision and Curriculum Development.

¤ † Kemp, Max. 1989. *Watching Children Read and Write: Observational Records for Children with Special Needs.* Portsmouth, NH: Heinemann.

‡ King, Martha L. December, 1975. "Language: Insights from acquisition." *Theory into Practice* 14: 293-298.

‡ Klima, Edward S. and Ursula Bellugi-Klima. 1966. "Syntactic regularities in the speech of children." *Psycholinguistic Papers*, 183-208. J. Lyons and R. J. Wales, eds. Edinburgh: Edinburgh University Press.

* Koch, Kenneth. 1973. *Rose, Where Did You Get that Red?: Teaching Great Poetry to Children*. New York: Random House.

‡ Laminack, Lester L. 1991. *Learning with Zachary*. Richmond Hill, ON: Scholastic.

+ Manning, Gary and Debbie, eds. 1989. *Whole Language: Beliefs and Practice, K-8*. Washington, DC: National Education Association.

¤ McConaghy, June. 1990. *Children Learning Through Literature: A Teacher Researcher Study*. Portsmouth, NH: Heinemann.

+ Monson, Robert J. and Michele M. Pahl. March, 1991. "Charting a New Course with Whole Language." *Educational Leadership* 48: 51-53.

^ Moss, Joy F. 1984. *Focus Units in Literature: A Handbook for Elementary School Teachers*. Urbana, IL: National Council of Teachers of English.

^ * Murphy, Richard. 1974. *Imaginary Worlds: Notes on a New Curriculum*. New York: Teachers & Writers Collaborative.

¤ ‡ Newkirk, Thomas. 1989. *More Than Stories: The Range of Children's Writing*. Portsmouth, NH: Heinemann.

¤ Newkirk, Thomas and Nancie Atwell, eds. 1988. *Understanding Writing: Ways of Observing, Learning, and Teaching*. 2nd ed. Portsmouth, NH: Heinemann.

‡ Newman, Judith M. 1984. *The Craft of Children's Writing*. Richmond Hill, ON: Scholastic. [Also Heinemann in USA]

‡ ——. 1985. "Insights from recent reading and writing research and their implications for developing whole language curriculum." *Whole Language: Theory in Use*, 7-36. Judith M. Newman, ed. Portsmouth, NH: Heinemann.

¤ ‡ ——, ed. 1985. *Whole Language: Theory in Use*. Portsmouth, NH: Heinemann.

+ Newman, Judith and Susan M. Church. September, 1990. "Myths of whole language." *The Reading Teacher* 44: 20-26.

¤ ——. 1990. *Finding Our Own Way: Teachers Exploring their Assumptions*. Portsmouth, NH: Heinemann.

¤ + Pace, Glennellen. January, 1991. "When teachers use literature for literacy instruction: Ways that constrain, ways that free." *Language Arts* 68: 12-25.

* Paterson, Katherine. 1981. *Gates of Excellence: On Reading and Writing Books for Children.* New York: Dutton.

¤ Peetoom, Adrian. 1986. *Shared Reading: Safe Risks with Whole Books.* Richmond Hill, ON: Scholastic.

Peterson, Mary. Spring, 1987. "A ghostly evening." *The Michigan Reading Journal* 20: 9-23.

¤ Peterson, Ralph. 1992. *Life in a Crowded Place: Making a Learning Community.* Portsmouth, NH: Heinemann. [Scholastic in Canada]

¤ † ° Peterson, Ralph and Maryann Eeds. *Grand Conversations: Literature Groups in Action.* Richmond Hill, ON: Scholastic. [Also Heinemann in USA]

¤ † Picciotto, Linda Pierce. 1992. *Evaluation: A Team Effort.* Richmond Hill, ON: Scholastic.

Raines, Shirley C. and Robert J. Canady. 1989. *Story S-t-r-e-t-c-h-e-r-s: Activities to Expand Children's Favorite Books.* Mt. Ranier, MD: Gryphon House.

‡ Read, Charles. 1975. *Children's Categorization of Speech Sounds in English.* Research report No. 17. Urbana, IL: National Council of Teachers of English.

¤ † Rhodes, Lynn. 1992. *Literacy Assessment. A Handbook of Instruments.* Portsmouth, NH: Heinemann.

¤ † Rhodes, Lynn and Nancy Shanklin. 1992. *Windows into Literacy: Assessing Learners K-8.* Portsmouth, NH: Heinemann.

+ Rich, Sharon J. November, 1985. "Restoring power to teachers: The impact of 'whole language.'" *Language Arts* 62: 717-24.

Rico, Gabriele Lusser. 1983. *Writing the Natural Way.* Los Angeles: J.P. Tarcher. [Distributed by Houghton Mifflin]

Rosenblatt, Louise. 1938. *Literature as Exploration.* New York: D. Appleton-Century. Reprinted in 1983 by the Modern Language Association, New York.

———. 1978. *The Reader, the Text, the Poem: The Transactional Theory of the Literary Work.* Carbondale, IL: Southern Illinois University Press.

Routman, Regie. 1988. *Transitions: From Literature to Literacy.* Portsmouth, NH: Heinemann.

° ¤ † + ———. 1991. *Invitations: Changing as Teachers and Learners K-12.* Portsmouth, NH: Heinemann.

‡ Sampson, Michael R., ed. 1986. *The Pursuit of Literacy: Early Reading and Writing*. Dubuque, IA: Kendall Hunt Publishing Company.

¤ † Sharp, Q.Q. 1989. *Evaluation: Whole Language Checklists for Evaluating Your Children, For Grades K-6*. New York: Scholastic.

¤ + Short, Kathy Gnagey and Carolyn Burke. 1991. *Creating Curriculum: Teachers and Students as a Community of Learners*. Portsmouth, NH: Heinemann.

¤ Short, Kathy Gnagey and Kathryn Mitchell Pierce, eds. 1990. *Talking About Books: Creating Literate Communities*. Portsmouth, NH: Heinemann.

Smith, Frank. 1973. *Psycholinguistics and Reading*. New York: Holt, Rinehart and Winston.

———, ed. 1975. *Comprehension and Learning*. Katonah, NY: Richard C. Owen.

———. 1979, 1985. *Reading Without Nonsense*. New York: Teachers College Press.

+ ———. January, 1981. "Demonstrations, engagement, and sensitivity: A revised approach to language learning." *Language Arts* 58: 103-112.

+ ———. September, 1981. "Demonstrations, engagement, and sensitivity: The choice between people and programs." *Language Arts* 58: 634-642.

‡ ———. 1983. *Essays into Literacy*. Portsmouth, NH: Heinemann.

* ———. 1988. *Insult to Intelligence: The Bureaucratic Invasion of Our Classrooms*. Portsmouth, NH: Heinemann. Originally published in 1986 by Arbor House.

+ ———. 1988. *Joining the Literacy Club: Further Essays into Education*. Portsmouth, NH: Heinemann.

———. 1988. *Understanding Reading*. 4th ed. Hillsdale, NJ: Erlbaum.

^ Spann, Sylvia and Mary Beth Culp, eds. 1975. *Thematic Units in Teaching English and the Humanities*. Urbana, IL: National Council of Teachers of English.

^ ———, eds. 1977. *Thematic Units in Teaching English and the Humanities: First Supplement*. Urbana, IL: National Council of Teachers of English.

+ Stephens, Diane. 1991. *Research on Whole Language: Support for a New Curriculum*. Katonah, NY: Richard C. Owen.

* Swartz, Larry. 1988. *Dramathemes*. Markham, ON: Pembroke. [Heinemann in USA]

\+ Taylor, D. November, 1989. "Toward a unified theory of literacy learning and instructional practices." *Phi Delta Kappan* 71: 184-193.

¤ † ———. February, 1990. "Teaching without testing: Assessing the complexity of children's literacy learning." *English Education* 22: 4-74.

———. 1991. *Learning Denied*. Portsmouth, NH: Heinemann.

‡ Taylor, D. and C. Dorsey-Gaines. 1988. *Growing Up Literate: Learning from Inner City Families*. Portsmouth, NH: Heinemann.

‡ Teale, William H. September, 1982. "Toward a theory of how children learn to read and write naturally." *Language Arts* 59: 550-570.

‡ Temple, Charles, Ruth Nathan, Frances Temple and Nancy Burris. 1993. *The Beginnings of Writing*. 3rd ed. Boston: Allyn and Bacon.

¤ † Tierney, Robert J., Mark A. Carter and Laura E. Desai. 1991. *Portfolio Assessment in the Reading-Writing Classroom*. Norwood, MA: Christopher-Gordon.

\+ Unsworth, Len. June, 1988. "Whole language or procedural display? The social context of popular whole language activities." *Australian Journal of Reading* 11: 127-137.

¤ Von Dras, Joan. 1990. "Transitions toward an integrated curriculum." *Talking About Books: Creating Literate Communities*, 121-133. Kathy Gnagey Short and Kathryn Mitchell Pierce, eds. Portsmouth, NH: Heinemann.

Vygotsky, Lev. S. 1978. *Mind in Society: The Development of Higher Psychological Processes*. Michael Cole, Vera John-Steiner, Sylvia Scribner and Ellen Souberman, eds. Cambridge, MA: Harvard University Press.

———. 1986. *Thought and Language*. Revised edition. A. Kozulin, ed. Cambridge, MA: MIT Press.

Wadsworth, Barry J. 1989. *Piaget's Theory of Cognitive and Affective Development*. New York: Longman.

° Watson, Dorothy J., ed. 1987. *Ideas and Insights: Language Arts in the Elementary School*. Urbana, IL: National Council of Teachers of English.

\+ ———. November, 1989. "Defining and describing whole language." *The Elementary School Journal* 90: 130-141.

+ Watson, Dorothy J., Carolyn L. Burke and Jerome C. Harste. 1989. *Whole Language: Inquiring Voices*. Richmond Hill, ON: Scholastic.

Weaver, Constance. 1980. *Psycholinguistics and Reading: From Process to Practice*. Cambridge, MA: Winthrop.

^ ——, ed. 1981. *Using Junior Novels to Develop Language and Thought: Five Integrative Teaching Guides*. Urbana, IL: National Council of Teachers of English.

¤ † ——. 1988. *Reading Process and Practice: From Socio-psycholinguistics to Whole Language*. Portsmouth, NH: Heinemann.

¤ * + †——. 1990. *Understanding Whole Language: From Principles to Practice*. Portsmouth, NH: Heinemann.

¤ + White, Connie. 1990. *Jevon Doesn't Sit at the Back Anymore*. Richmond Hill, ON: Scholastic.

Winograd, Peter N., Karen K. Wixson and Marjorie Y. Lipson, eds. 1989. *Improving Basal Reading Instruction*. New York: Teachers College Press.

Zarrillo, James. October, 1989. "Teachers' interpretations of literature-based reading." *The Reading Teacher* 43: 23-28.

Appendix 1

~ ~ ~ ~ ~ ~ ~ ~ ~ ~

What is whole language?

~ ~ ~ ~ ~

There are some definable differences between the roles of teacher and students in what many people refer to as the "transmission" mode of teaching/learning and those same roles in a whole language classroom where the "transactional" mode of teaching/learning is prevalent. Our purpose in this appendix is to summarize some of those differences. (See also "Whole language principles as goals," pages 31-44.)

Learning and the learner

Transmission mode

The learner passively and often begrudgingly practices skills, memorizes facts, and accumulates information.

Material produced and learned is rarely perceived by the learner as functional or purposeful.

Uniform instruction reflects the assumption that all learners learn the same things at the same time.

Transactional mode

The learner actively and often enthusiastically engages in complex language and reasoning processes, and in the construction of complex concepts.

Authentic experiences and projects are typically perceived by the learner as functional and purposeful.

Learner-sensitive instruction is based on the explicit assumption that all learners learn and develop uniquely.

The learner's lack of adult correctness generates negative feedback to what are considered "errors" in execution.

The learner is given freedom to experiment and risk without fear of negative feedback, in the expectation that a gradual approach to adult correctness will occur.

Competition is seen as the best incentive for learning.

Collaboration is seen as the best facilitator of learning.

Nature and development of the curriculum

Transmission mode

The curriculum emphasizes minimal skills and factual information.

The curriculum is divided into subjects, and the subjects are divided into skills and facts; language and literacy are taught as mastery of the isolated skills.

The curriculum is determined by outside forces: curriculum guides and objectives, texts and programs, etc.

Reading materials are characterized at the earliest levels by unnaturally stilted language ("basalese") that consists of basic sight words and phonically regular words.

Beyond the primary grades, many reading selections consist of pieces that have been altered, abridged or excerpted from literary works.

Transactional mode

The curriculum encourages the kinds of learning experiences that lifelong learners engage in outside of school.

The curriculum is integrated around topics and themes, with emphasis on the development of language and literacy skills "across the curriculum."

The curriculum is decided by and negotiated among the teacher and the students.

Reading materials at the earliest levels include a wide variety of materials in natural language patterns, with an emphasis on predictable and repetitive patterns.

Beyond the primary grades, both the range and depth of reading materials is increased, with an emphasis on whole works of high literary quality and appropriate nonfiction prose.

Direct teaching of skills occurs in isolation, according to a predetermined teach/practice/test format, with attention to helping learners master specific parts of language.

Direct teaching of skills occurs within the context of the whole learning experience and the learners' needs and interests; language is learned in the context of whole pieces of literature.

Teacher roles in facilitating learning

Transmission mode

The teacher dispenses information, assigns tasks, and evaluates student work.

The teacher determines what work must be done, and explains lessons and assignments.

The teacher creates a climate in which competition and comparison are encouraged.

The teacher treats students as incapable and deficient insofar as they have not measured up to preset objectives and/or norms.

The teacher penalizes errors, thus discouraging risk-taking and individual thinking (hypothesis formation).

Transactional mode

The teacher serves as a role model, demonstrating what it means to be a literate person and a lifelong learner.

The teacher stimulates learning, both directly and indirectly; rather than assigning the same work to all students, he or she suggests possibilities for individual or collaborative learning experiences.

The teacher creates a supportive community of learners in which collaboration and mutual assistance are encouraged.

The teacher treats students as capable and developing, honoring their unique patterns of development and offering invitations and challenges to their individual growth.

The teacher responds positively to successive approximations, thus encouraging risk-taking and thinking.

The teacher fosters dependence on external authority to determine what to do and how to do things, and to decide what is and isn't correct.

The teacher shares responsibility for curricular decision-making with the students, thus empowering them to take ownership of and responsibility for their own learning.

Assessment and evaluation

Transmission mode

Evaluation is often based on a single assessment (e.g., a standardized test score).

Assessment is infrequent.

The learner is assessed in the performance of relatively unnatural tasks (e.g., multiple-choice tests).

Only "objective" scores are used for assessment and evaluation.

The curriculum evaluates both the teacher and the students.

Assessment is primarily norm-referenced or criterion-referenced.

Transactional mode

Evaluation is based on numerous assessments of various kinds.

Assessment is ongoing and continuous.

The learner is observed and assessed while engaging in authentic literacy and learning experiences.

The subjective judgment of the teacher is crucial, as is self-evaluation by the learner.

Both the teacher and the students evaluate the curriculum: their shared learning experiences.

Assessment is primarily learner-referenced.

A continuum from traditional to whole language teaching

Moving from a transmission mode of teaching to a transactional one isn't usually an easy or instantaneous change of direction. Teachers may find themselves anywhere along the reading continuum outlined on page 211, or the more general one shown on page 212.

Transmission mode ————————▶ *Transactional mode*		
Both content and method reflect a transmission model.	Content reflects a transactional model, while method reflects a transmission model.	Both content and method reflect a transactional model.
Reading is seen as reproducing the words on the page.	Reading is seen as getting meaning from the words on the page.	Reading is seen as constructing meaning.
Reading is taught as a sequence of isolated skills that have to be mastered.	Reading is taught as a set of strategies (e.g., predicting, then confirming and correcting) that can be consciously learned and adopted (metacognition).	The development of reading strategies is encouraged through teacher "demonstrations," student and/or student/teacher conferences, group mini-lessons and literature group discussions.
Skills are taught from a prepackaged program in a teach/practice/test format.	The teacher models skills and strategies, and the students practice them; they may be tested.	During authentic reading experiences, the students are reminded to apply learned strategies, and are given help as needed.
The program is the authority; the teacher is a technician.	The teacher is the authority.	The students are also authorities; the teacher helps them to recognize and make more effective use of what they already know.
The emphasis is on testing and evaluating the students.	The emphasis is on teaching (modeling for) the students.	The emphasis is on the students' learning; the teacher simply assists.

Reading			
Basal program with some modifications: selected use of workbook pages and stories, reading aloud to the students, providing sustained silent reading or DEAR time, etc.	Mini-lessons on strategies in the teach/practice/test format	Mini-lessons offered as demonstrations and invitations	Strategies discussed as needed within conferences or literature group discussions
Writing			
Students writing personal narratives	Mini-lessons on specific writing conventions	Mini-lessons drawn from children's literature	Immersion in whole works of literature during reading/writing workshops, leading to the writing of more significant works in more genres
Literature			
Adapted or whole pieces of literature to which students respond through a mixture of content questions and more sophisticated questions requiring higher-order reasoning and divergent thinking	Individual works of literature that serve as "core" resources for various across-the-curriculum activities	Programs involving a wide range of literature	Authentic literature experiences, demonstrated and invited through reading aloud, reading/writing workshops, literature discussion groups, experiencing literature through oral language, wide reading of literature across the curriculum, etc.
Theme study			
Teaching of "skills" across the curriculum	Meaningful, teacher-directed activities on a specific topic of study (theme unit)	Broad teacher-chosen topic initiates subsequent student choices (theme exploration)	Teacher and students together negotiate topics and develop questions for individual and collaborative discovery (theme cycles)

Appendix 2

~ ~ ~ ~ ~ ~ ~ ~ ~ ~

The fourth-graders' play

~ ~ ~ ~ ~ ~

FAMILY PROBLEMS

By Amanda, Brandy, Brian, Jeni, Jenny, Jill, Lisa, Maria and Melissa

Scene 1: The family at home . . .

[Mom stumbles into a table because she's had too much vodka to drink. She has just lost her job because of her drinking problem. She gets a Kleenex from a box on the table.]

MOM: I'm so stupid! I lost my job!!! [She sits in an easy chair, sobbing.]

[Kids walk in with their friend Maria. They see their mom crying and are embarrassed because their friend is there.]

MARIA: [whispering] Why is your mom crying?

JENNY: I don't know.

LISA: Mom, why are you crying?

MOM: Shut up!!!

KIDS: Sorry!!

[The kids sit down on the couch in front of the TV. Dad walks in and puts his briefcase on the table. He's holding something — an empty Sprite bottle — behind his back.]

DAD: Connie, have you been drinking again?

MOTHER: No, I haven't, Robert, for your information!!!

DAD: [yelling] You *have* been drinking. I found vodka in this Sprite bottle!! [He practically shoves the bottle in her face.]

MOM: Why don't you just leave me alone, it's my life! [She sits down on the couch where the kids are watching TV.]

JENNY: Can we go outside to play?

DAD: Shut up, I'm trying to think.

LISA: Maria, I think you better go home!

MARIA: OK. I'll see you tomorrow. [She exits, talking to herself.] I hope they're going to be all right!

Scene 2: The next day, on the playground at school . . .

[The scene opens with the two abused kids on the playground, sitting on the swings talking. Jenny has a large bruise on her arm.]

JENNY: Dad sure was in a bad mood yesterday.

LISA: *Now* what did he do to give you that bruise?

JENNY: He hit me [rubs it gently]. It hurts.

[Two teenagers enter.]

AMANDA: You guys look like you're down.

BRANDY: Yeah, man, what's wrong?

AMANDA: Ya wanna get high?

BRANDY: We got somethin' that will really make ya feel good.

AMANDA: How 'bout some, man.

JENNY: *No thanks.*

LISA: We learned at school that drugs aren't good for us.

BRANDY: Those teachers don't know anything, don't listen to them, man.

JENNY: I still don't want any.

LISA: Me either.

AMANDA: You guys are pretty uncool.

BRANDY: You guys have a pretty low life.

AMANDA AND BRANDY: See ya, man!

[Exit]

JENNY: After all our troubles at home, look what we get here.

LISA: Yeah, I know what you mean.

JENNY: Maybe we should run away.

LISA: Yeah, 'cause Dad really hurts us when he hits us.

JENNY: Let's go!

[The girls jump off the swings and walk away.]

Scene 3: *That same night, at home . . .*

[The two kids are packing to run away from home. They pack things like food, some money, and the other things mentioned below. They stuff these things in a backpack and a duffel bag, the kind used for gym.]

LISA: Let's see, we've got some food and some money: we sure didn't have very much in our banks, though! What else do we need?

JENNY: We'd better take some blankets to keep warm.

LISA: Yeah!

JENNY: And maybe some clean clothes.

LISA: Okay. How about something to play with?

JENNY: Well, I guess so, if it's small enough to fit into the backpack. Let's take a book to read, too.

LISA: Okay . . . I think I'll take *Cracker Jackson.* His babysitter Alma must feel just like us, the way she was abused by her husband!

JENNY: Yeah.

LISA: Do you think we should write a note to Mom and Dad, so they won't worry so much?

JENNY: Yeah, maybe so. But we better hurry up and leave, before they hear us.

LISA: Okay. But where are we going to go?

JENNY: We could go to the playground just for tonight. We can sleep in the tunnels, so it's not so windy. And then tomorrow we can find someplace else to stay.

LISA: Okay. We'd better hurry, 'cause I think I hear Dad coming.

Scene 4: *The very next day . . .*

[It's the afternoon of the next day, when Dad has returned home from work. Mom and Dad are in the middle of an argument. She's sitting on the arm of the easy chair and he's standing close by.]

MOM: I *told* you, I *wasn't* drinking. I just had a little vodka.

DAD: Yes, you were, Connie, admit it! You already totaled the car last month, and we don't have the money for another clunker.

MOM: Never mind about that. We need to find Lisa and Jenny before they get into trouble. Look at this note I found while you were at work. It says, "We ran away because you're abusing us by hitting us and being drunk and neglecting us almost every day. Don't try to find us, because we won't come home ever again. We have enough supplies to live away from home. Goodbye. Lisa, Jenny."

DAD: Don't try to change the subject, Connie, you *were* drinking.

MOM: We can talk about that after we find the children.

DAD: No, we'll talk about it *now*.

MOM: I told you I wasn't drinking.

DAD: Yes, you were. The children said you were, in the letter, and you totaled the car when you were drunk, and you're drunk now, too.

MOM: I don't care what the children said, I was not — I repeat, *was not* — drunk when I had that accident. That guy ran into me, I didn't hit him.

DAD: It doesn't matter if you hit him or he hit you, *you* were drunk. And you should have been watching where you were going.

MOM: I *was* watching where I was going. I told you, he hit me, it wasn't my fault.

DAD: Yeah, sure, Connie, why do you think the children ran away?

MOM: Because you've been beatin' on them all the time, that's why, *Robert*.

DAD: That's a bunch of bull, I've never hit those brats.

MOM: You beat those so-called brats all the time.

DAD: Do not.

MOM: Yes, you do.

DAD: Don't.

MOM: Do.

DAD: If you don't shut up, I'll . . .

[He pushes her off the arm of the easy chair and into the chair itself, then starts choking her.]

MOM: I don't care if I am drunk, I just want to find my precious

little babies. [She gets free of him and rushes toward the door.]
Goodbye!

DAD: You'd better take your vodka bottle with you so you don't get sick.

[He throws the bottle on the floor hard, in the direction of the mother.]

Scene 5: A week later, in the park . . .

[The daughters have run out of money, so they're stealing food out of the garbage cans at a restaurant. As the scene opens, they are running away from a man who is chasing them because they've gotten into his garbage cans. Out of breath, they stop behind some other garbage cans.]

LISA: Do you think he's gone yet?

JENNY: I think so. What did you get before he started chasing us?

LISA: I got part of a chicken leg. What about you?

JENNY: I didn't even find anything worth stealing.

LISA: Oh, I hate it [almost starting to cry]. I don't like having to eat left-over food out of people's garbage. And it's cold sleeping in the park. I wish we'd found someplace else to stay.

JENNY: I know.

[Jenny puts her arm around Lisa and they sit there for a minute.]

JENNY: Well, we'd better look somplace else for some food.

[She gets up, then reaches down to help Lisa up. As soon as they start walking, they see the two older kids who tried to sell them drugs on the playground at school.]

BRANDY: Hey, so we meet again!

JENNY: I guess so [in a shaky voice].

AMANDA: Ya want some, this time?

BRANDY: Ah, you can't handle it, can you?

AMANDA: You guys are just babies.

JENNY: We are not babies.

LISA: Fine, we'll take it!

BRANDY: Hey, maybe you guys aren't babies after all!

AMANDA: Here, have some grass, man!

BRANDY: It's RAD!

[One of the drug dealers lights a marijuana cigarette, the two drug dealers each take a puff and then they pass the joint to the girls. They each take a puff, and the joint is passed around again. Seeing that the girls are getting high, the drug dealers laugh and leave.]

LISA: Gee, I feel better.

JENNY: Me too. We can wait until later to get some food.

Scene 6: Yet another week later . . .

[The girls are sitting in the park, since that's where they've been sleeping. They are taking turns with a joint and are obviously already high on marijuana. Their friend Maria comes up to them.]

MARIA: I found you at last! You've been gone two weeks already!!

LISA: Who are you?

JENNY: Yeah, who are you?

MARIA: You know who I am! [She is alarmed.]

LISA: Then who are you? [She speaks kind of smarty.]

MARIA: I'm your best friend! Maria!

[Jenny offers the cigarette to Maria!]

MARIA: No thanks! You guys are really messed up!

LISA: We aren't messed up, you are!

MARIA: Will you guys come home? Pleeease?

JENNY: Who do you think you are, coming here and telling us what to do and where to go?

MARIA: I'm not telling you what to do. I'm just asking you to come home.

LISA: Leave us alone, and go home yourself!

JENNY: Yeah! Leave us alone, you have no business being here!

[Starting to cry, Maria gets up and starts running away.]

Scene 7: Meanwhile, at the counseling office . . .

[The girls' mother has decided to try to get help for her alcoholism and for the problem of her husband beating her and the kids — when they're home. She walks into the counselors' office. The two counselors are seated behind a desk. Mom walks in very embarrassed and scared. Mrs. Schroeder, one of the counselors, is looking at some files.]

MOM: Excuse me, I'm Connie. I'd like to see Mrs. Schroeder. I have an appointment.

MRS. SCHROEDER: Hello, I'm Mrs. Schroeder, and this is Mrs. Campbell. Please have a seat.

[The two counselors gesture for Connie to sit down.]

MRS. SCHROEDER: So why don't you tell us about yourself, and what your problem is.

MOM: My problem is . . . [She thinks a minute.]

MRS. CAMPBELL: [reassuringly] It's okay.

MOM: My problem is that my two kids have run away, and my husband beats me because I drink too much.

MRS. SCHROEDER: Oooh, that must be hard on you.

MOM: Yes, it's very hard on me. [Pause] Do you think you could help me?

MRS. CAMPBELL: Yes, I'm sure we can help you.

MOM: [all in a rush] I can't stop drinking. I've tried, but last month I totaled the car, and it cost too much to have it fixed, and we don't have another car . . . Are you sure you can help me?

MRS. SCHROEDER: Yes, I'm sure. For one thing, we could take you to AA with us.

MOM: Alcoholics Anonymous?

MRS. CAMPBELL: Yes. You'd meet a lot of people with problems just like yours. I'm sure they can help you solve your drinking problem.

MOM: I'll think about it. [After a pause, she gets up to leave.] Well, thank you very much.

MRS. SCHROEDER: Will you be back for another session tomorrow?

MOM: Yes, probably. Thank you.

MRS. CAMPBELL: See you tomorrow. Bye.

MOM: Bye.

Scene 8: In the park, yet another week later . . .

[It's early in the morning. Maria finds the sisters as they are just waking up and getting out of their tunnel. The girls rub their eyes to wake up, and rub their arms to get warm.]

MARIA: I've got a place for you guys to stay.

LISA: Is it warm?

JENNY: Will it help us get off drugs?

MARIA: You guys can go to a counselor.

LISA: What good will that do? A counselor isn't going to give us a place to live, is she?

MARIA: You guys can go to The Ark and stay for fourteen days.

JENNY: But what if they make us go back home?

LISA: Yeah, we don't want to do that. Mom is drunk all the time, and Dad beats us.

MARIA: Come on, you guys.

LISA: We're scared to go.

JENNY: What is The Ark, and where is it, anyway?

MARIA: It's a place where older kids and teenagers can go to spend some time and get help for their problems.

LISA: Are we old enough to go there?

MARIA: I think so. How old are you?

JENNY: Lisa just turned twelve, and I'm almost fourteen.

MARIA: Yeah, you're old enough.

LISA: When can we go?

MARIA: As soon as you want. And they can help you get off drugs, too.

JENNY: Can they help us with our mom and dad?

MARIA: Maybe!

LISA: Okay, let's go see.

Scene 9: After a night at the Ark, the girls return home . . .

[The mother is seated in the easy chair and the father on the couch; both are reading as the girls enter.]

JENNY: Mom, Dad . . .

MOM: Thank goodness you're home! We love you two so much!

[Jenny sits on the arm of the chair nearest the couch; Lisa stands by the other side of the chair; the father walks over toward the girls.]

DAD: Why did you run away?

JENNY: We ran away because you beat us, and Mom drinks too much.

LISA: We stayed at this place called The Ark.

JENNY: Yeah! We met these neat ladies named Mrs. Schroeder and Mrs. Campbell.

MOM: Mrs. Schroeder and Mrs. Campbell? [She looks very surprised.]

LISA: They're waiting outside in their car.

MOM: Go get them and ask them if they would come talk to us for a miniute. [The girls leave.] Robert, Mrs. Schroeder and Mrs. Campbell have been helping me with my drinking problem.

[The girls and Mrs. Schroeder and Mrs. Campbell enter.]

MOM: Hello, Mrs. Schroeder and Mrs. Campbell.

LISA: Mom, you know them?

MOM: Yes, these two counselors have been helping me with my drinking problem.

MRS. SCHROEDER: That's right. The first step in recovery is admitting that you have a problem, and your mom is taking that step. Perhaps if we all work together we can help her deal with the problem of alcoholism.

ROBERT: I think I could use some help too. I do hit Lisa and Jenny a little bit.

MRS. CAMPBELL: That's the first important step. If you're willing, we're willing to help the family get back together, no matter what it takes.

MOM: Well, I'm ready.

[Dad moves closer and puts his arm on Mom's shoulder; Jenny slides off the edge of the chair, almost into her mother's lap, and Lisa does the same from the other side.]

Appendix 3

~ ~ ~ ~ ~ ~ ~ ~ ~

Selecting theme books

~ ~ ~ ~ ~ ~

Criteria for evaluating children's books

Picture books

Text

Narrative

~ Is the narrative both credible and inventive?
~ If it contains fantastic elements, does it help readers maintain a willing suspension of disbelief?
~ Is there a developed conflict that will interest young readers?

Characters

~ Are the characters well delineated?
~ Are they believable, interesting and free from racial and sexual stereotypes?

Style

~ Does the text use language inventively and artistically without condescending to a young audience?
~ At the same time, is the style appropriate for that audience?

Theme

~ Does the book develop a significant theme, one appropriate for its intended readers?

~ Does it avoid overt moralizing?

Illustrations

Visual Elements

~ Are the illustrations visually appealing and of high artistic quality?
~ Do they effectively use such elements as line, space, tone and color?
~ Do they accurately correspond to the content of the book?
~ Do they extend the text, providing additional information about the characters and plot?
~ Would the text be as effective without the illustrations?

Style and Design

~ Does the artist's choice of style and artistic media support the tone and content of the text?
~ Does the artistic style reflect the book's literary style?
~ Are the illustrations well integrated?
~ Does either text or illustrations overshadow the other?

Suitability and appeal

Suitability

~ Is the book as a whole appropriate for the ages and reading levels of a particular group of children?
~ Will it challenge those readers, providing them with new information or insights?
~ Will it encourage analytical thinking?

Appeal

~ Will the story and illustrations spark the interest of young readers?
~ Will it keep their attention?

Information books

Content

~ Is the subject adequately covered? Are any important facts omitted?

~ Are all facts accurate?
~ Is the information current, reflecting new advances or discoveries?
~ If the subject matter is controversial, are differing points of view presented?
~ Are fact and theory clearly distinguished?
~ Does the author appear to be knowledgeable and informed?

Illustrations

~ Are the illustrations of high quality or are they text-bookish?
~ Are they accurate?
~ Do they present information effectively, clarifying the text?
~ Is their style appropriate for the subject?
~ Are they overly distracting to the reader?

Organization

~ Is the book organized in a logical manner?
~ Is it written in a way that will interest reluctant readers?
~ If facts are presented as part of a narrative, is the factual material clear and well integrated?
~ Can a reader locate a particular piece of information easily?
~ Does the book contain aids to the reader: a glossary, a bibliography, maps, charts, an index?

Style

~ Is the language appropriate for the audience?
~ Are difficult terms explained directly or indirectly?
~ Is the style exciting and interesting, vivid and specific?

A sample collection: Snow and winter

The following annotated list reflects some of the books Joel and Nora had on hand or located for the group's weather theme exploration. (Cited titles are marked.)

Fantasy

Benson, Patrick. 1990. *Little Penguin*. New York: Philomel.

Pip, a three-year-old Adelie penguin, goes exploring. Through her friendship with a three-year-old sperm whale, she is eventually able to deal with the snobbish Emperor penguins. Simple language, repetition and detailed watercolor paintings make this an appealing book for beginning readers.

Harris, Dorothy Joan. 1987. *Four Seasons for Toby*. Illus. Vlasta van Kampen. Richmond Hill: Scholastic.

Towards the end of winter, Toby Turtle sets out to find spring. But his slow journey around the farmyard perimeter takes him through all four seasons before he finally returns to the snow-covered edge of his own pond. A gentle, informative look at the seasons.

Kroll, Stephen. 1987. *It's Groundhog Day!* New York: Holiday House. [Also Scholastic]

If spring comes early, Roland Raccoon will have to close his ski lodge, so he kidnaps Godfrey Groundhog to prevent him from seeing his shadow. One of very few books about Groundhog Day, this simple, seasonal story is humorous and will appeal to young readers.

Lawson, Robert. 1954. *The Tough Winter*. New York: Viking.

The animals of Rabbit Hill make it through a tough winter partly because of their attitude and partly by working together. They face fire, vicious dogs and near starvation, but through it all, Georgie, one of the rabbits, vows that he's "going to stay on the hill no matter what happens." (p.76) Sections of this short novel might be read aloud to the children.

* Lobel, Arnold. 1976. *Frog and Toad All Year*. New York: Harper & Row. [Also Scholastic]

Included among four seasonal stories involving friends Frog and Toad is one about winter. (See description on page 93.)

Loretan, Sylvia and Jan Lenica. 1988. *Bob the Snowman*. Switzerland: Bohem Press. [Also Scholastic]

This simple story demonstrates the water cycle. When Bob the snowman decides to go south like the birds, he soon turns into a puddle. But then the sun shines and Bob climbs into the sky, drop by drop, to become a cloud. The wind blows him back north and he falls again as snow, right where he started from.

Mendez, Phil. 1989. *The Black Snowman.* Illus. Carole Byard. New York: Scholastic.

Jacob and his brother make a snowman and wrap a scrap of cloth they find around it. But the cloth is really the remnant of a magical African storytelling shawl that makes this winter very special.

* Wood, Audrey. 1989. *Little Penguin's Tale.* San Diego: Harcourt Brace Jovanovich.

While Grand Nanny Penguin tells six little penguins a wild story, a seventh penguin wanders off and experiences everything she describes. Here, winter is wild, frantic and anything but dull. Bold, humorous illustrations set the book in a land of perpetual snow.

Folktales and literary folktales

Andersen, Hans Christian. 1982. *The Snow Queen.* Ed. Amy Ehrlich. Illus. Susan Jeffers. New York: Dial.

The classic tale of brave Gerda who must travel to the land of the Snow Queen to rescue her best friend Kai. Snow is an evil force in this story, but is ultimately vanquished by the coming of spring. Jeffers' pen-and-ink drawings effectively convey the mystery and awe of the Snow Queen's wintry world. See also Jeffers' illustrations in *Stopping by Woods on a Snowy Evening.*

de Gerez, Toni. 1986. *Louhi, Witch of North Farm.* Illus. Barbara Cooney. New York: Viking Kestrel.

A Finnish folktale adapted from the *Kalevala* about Louhi, a witch who steals the sun and moon and hides them behind nine great doors and locks on Copper Mountain. When the smith, Sepp, convinces her to return the stolen celestial objects, spring is able to come again. The flat, acrylic paintings by Barbara Cooney, two-time winner of the Caldecott Medal, contrast the desolation of a northern winter with the spring that follows it.

McDermott, Gerald. 1984. *Daughter of the Earth: A Roman Myth.* New York: Delacorte.

Award-winning illustrator Gerald McDermott retells the Roman myth of the abduction of Proserpina and the origin of winter. This is one of several tales that might invite children to create their own "pourquoi" tales about why we have winter.

Marshak, Samuel. 1983. *The Month Brothers: A Slavic Tale.* Trans. Thomas P. Whitney. Illus. Diane Stanley. New York: William Morrow.

One January a young girl is sent into a blizzard to find some flowers for her stepsister's birthday. Along the way she is helped by the twelve months. This Czechoslovakian folktale appeals to children because of its personification of the twelve months and, by extension, of the weather. Other variants of this tale include the Greek "The Twelve Months," in *Folktales of Greece*, and the Italian "The Months," in *The Fairy Ring*.

Realistic fiction

Bauer, Caroline Feller. 1987. *Midnight Snowman*. Illus. Caroline Stock. New York: Atheneum.

A group of children build an unusual snowman one night. This realistic book might be contrasted with Raymond Briggs' fantasy, *The Snowman*.

d'Aulaire, Ingri and Edgar Parin. 1939. *Children of the Northlights*. New York: Viking.

Two Lapp children experience winter life at the top of the world. The text is fairly complex, but it serves as a nice contrast to books like *Happy Winter*.

Goffstein, M.B. 1986. *Our Snowman*. New York: Harper & Row.

In simple language Goffstein tells how a girl teaches her younger brother to build a snowman. Illustrated with child-like pastel drawings, this book is a nice companion to Keats' *The Snowy Day*.

Hader, Berta and Elmer. 1948. *The Big Snow*. New York: Macmillan.

Winner of the Caldecott Medal, this book describes a snowstorm and its effect on various forest animals. Like *The Tough Winter*, it presents an animal's perspective on winter and a positive relationship between animals and human beings.

* Keats, Ezra Jack. 1962. *The Snowy Day*. New York: Viking. [Also Scholastic]

A description of this book, winner of the Caldecott Medal, is given on page 94.

San Soucci, Daniel. 1990. *North Country Night*. New York: Doubleday.

A contemporary tale similar to *The Big Snow*, this book describes the nocturnal activities of north country animals such as owls, coyotes, wolves and cottontails during a snowstorm. The paintings of animals and moonlit snow scenes are spectacular.

Tresselt, Alvin. 1947. *White Snow, Bright Snow.* Illus. Roger Duvoisin. New York: Lothrop. [Also Scholastic]

Winner of the Caldecott Medal, this book describes a snowstorm from its onset through its aftermath as it affects a small town. The stylized illustrations are childlike and simple, yet effective.

Zolotow, Charlotte. 1988. *Something Is Going to Happen.* Illus. Catherine Stock. New York: Harper & Row.

Yet another story about the first snowfall.

Wordless picture books

Briggs, Raymond. 1978. *The Snowman.* New York: Random House.

This winner of the Boston Globe-Horn Book Award tells about a boy's fanciful adventures with a snowman who comes to life one evening. The pencil drawings depict both a snowman's initiation into the domestic world of electrical appliances, make-up and clothing and a young boy's journey into a fantasy world. This wordless book has also been made into an award-winning film that is available on videotape.

McCully, Emily Arnold. 1985. *First Snow.* New York: Harper & Row.

A family of mice goes on a sledding trip and skate on a pond. The watercolor illustrations are appealing and provide ample opportunities for readers to create their own texts.

Information books

Branley, Franklin M. 1986. *Snow Is Falling.* Illus. Holly Keller. Rev. ed. New York: Harper & Row.

Typical of Branley's many weather books for children, this one discusses the reasons snow is important to animals, the dangers of snow, and the mysteries of a snowflake. It is less technical than some of his others and easier to read by first-graders.

Webster, David. 1968. *Snow Stumpers.* New York: Museum of Natural History Press.

This book poses questions about a number of photographs of snow scenes. For example: what causes frost crystals to form on car windows? and then later answers them. It also includes snow experiments such as "Melting Snow," "Making a Snow Gauge" and "Snow Lights."

Williams, Terry Tempest and Ted Major. 1984. *The Secret Language of Snow.* San Francisco: Sierra Club/Pantheon.

Intended for older readers, this book is a good resource, describing the many different kinds of snow as seen through the eyes of the Inuits.

Biography

Kurelek, William. 1973. *A Prairie Boy's Winter*. Montreal: Tundra.

This is a Canadian Library Association Best Illustrated Book. In it, renowned Canadian artist William Kurelek recounts his life on the Canadian Prairie as a child, from the first snowfall to the return of the first crow, through paintings accompanied by short personal narratives. These include excellent descriptions of winter games, such as Fox and Geese and ice hockey (with homemade equipment).

* Wilder, Laura Ingalls. 1940. *The Long Winter*. New York: Harper & Row. [Also Scholastic]

The most intense of Wilder's "Little House" series, this book would appeal more to older readers, though small sections describing the many blizzards the family endured could be read to younger children. Chapter 9, in which Laura and her schoolmates must walk home in a blinding blizzard, is especially good.

Poetry anthologies

Bauer, Caroline Feller, ed. 1986. *Snowy Day: Stories and Poems*. Illus. Margot Tomes. New York: Lippincott.

This book, itself an exercise in theme exploration, contains 28 poems about snow, including Dennis Lee's "Lying on Things," X.J. Kennedy's "Moonwalk" and Ogden Nash's "Winter Morning." Bauer also presents three folktales about snow, some factual information, instructions for snow-related crafts, and some recipes, along with a good bibliography of other snow-related books. See also her companion volume, *Rainy Day Stories and Poems*.

* de Regniers, Beatrice Schenk et al. 1988. *Sing a Song of Popcorn: Every Child's Book of Poems*. Illus. Marcia Brown, et al. New York: Scholastic.

This colorful anthology, illustrated by a number of award-winning artists, has a section called "Mostly Weather" with art by Marcia Brown. Several of the poems deal with snow and winter.

Frank, Josette, ed. 1990. *Snow Toward Evening: A Year in a River Valley.* Illus. Thomas Locker. New York: Dial.

Twelve nature poems by writers such as Christina Rossetti and Langston Hughes are illustrated with exquisite oil paintings. The poems for January, February and December deal with snow and winter and are accessible to young readers.

* Prelutsky, Jack. 1984. *It's Snowing, It's Snowing.* Illus. Jeanne Titherington. New York: Greenwillow.

Seventeen poems about snow detail a variety of snow-related experiences. "The Snowman's Lament" makes a nice companion piece to Briggs' *The Snowman.* Most of the poems are humorous, capturing experiences common to many children.

* Prelutsky, Jack. 1988. *Read-Aloud Rhymes for the Very Young.* Illus. Marc Brown. New York: Alfred A. Knopf.

This excellent anthology of short rhymes includes several pages of snow poems such as David McCord's "Snowman," Karla Kuskin's "Snow" and Maurice Sendak's "January." Most are easily read by young children.

Individual poems

Frost, Robert. 1978. *Stopping By Woods on a Snowy Evening.* Illus. Susan Jeffers. New York: Dutton.

Frost's famous poem appeals to young readers in this version, primarily because of the detailed pen-and-ink drawings of a man caught in a winter storm. Even first-graders can sense the mystery of the snowy woods conveyed by the poem.

* Gundersheimer, Karen. 1982. *Happy Winter.* New York: Harper & Row.

This rhyming story focuses mainly on indoor activities during winter weather. It is a bright, positive look at snow, lacking the pathos of *The Snowy Day.* It also includes a recipe "Happy Winter Fudge Cake."